DUBLIN
THE MAKING OF A
MEDIEVAL CITY

D1597286

Authors

Dr Howard B. Clarke FRHistS combined lifelong interests in medieval history and archaeology as a founder member and former chairman of the Friends of Medieval Dublin. In 1991 he became a director of The Medieval Trust, the parent body of Dublinia Ltd, which opened its medieval exhibition to the public in 1993. He is the author of a complementary fascicle of the *Royal Irish Academy's Irish Historic Towns Atlas, Dublin, part I, to 1610*, along with numerous articles in historical works. He has also edited and joint-edited a number of publications, among them *Medieval Dublin* (two volumes), *Irish Cities*, *Ireland and Scandinavia in the Early Viking Age* and *The Vikings in Ireland and Beyond*.

Sarah Dent graduated in archaeology and ancient history from Newcastle University, having worked on a Roman site at South Shields. She specialised in the role of heritage centres in the Irish tourism industry. Former curator and education officer at Dublinia, she devised a programme for third-level students, school workshops and outreach visits. She played a leading role in the redesign of the exhibition in 2001, creating an interactive archaeology room. She is former director of the Irish Young Archaeologists' Club.

Dr Ruth Johnson is an archaeologist specialising in Viking, medieval and urban archaeology. Ruth has been the Dublin City Archaeologist since 2001 where she oversees the protection, management and promotion of Dublin City's archaeological resource. Formerly the curator of Dublinia, she is a licence-eligible archaeologist with a BA from the Institute of Archaeology, University College London and a PhD in medieval history from Trinity College Dublin. She is the author of several books including *Viking Age Dublin*, co-author of *Dublin and the Viking World* and joint-editor of *The Vikings in Ireland and Beyond*.

DUBLIN
THE MAKING OF A
MEDIEVAL CITY

Howard B. Clarke,
Sarah Dent and Ruth Johnson

Comhairle Cathrach
Bhaile Átha Cliath
Dublin City Council

An Chomhairle Oidhreachta
The Heritage Council

THE O'BRIEN PRESS
DUBLIN

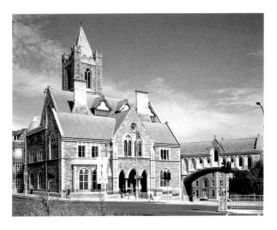

Dublinia and bridge to Christ Church Cathedral.

This updated edition first published 2019 by The O'Brien Press Ltd,
12 Terenure Road East, Rathgar, Dublin 6, D06 HD27, Ireland.
Tel: +353 1 4923333; Fax: +353 1 4922777
E-mail: books@obrien.ie
Website: www.obrien.ie
First published 2002 as "Dublinia: The Story of Medieval Dublin".
The O'Brien Press is a member of Publishing Ireland.

ISBN: 978-1-78849-120-4

Copyright for text © The Medieval Trust
Copyright for typesetting, layout, editing, design © The O'Brien Press Ltd

All rights reserved. No part of this publication may be reproduced or utilised in any form
or by any means, electronic or mechanical, including photocopying, recording or in any information
storage and retrieval system, without permission in writing from the publisher.

1 3 5 4 2
19 21 23 22 20

Editing: The O'Brien Press Ltd.
Typesetting, layout and design, including cover design: Anú Design, Tara
Front cover illustrations:
Top: The Marriage of Aífe and Strongbow by Daniel Maclise, The National Gallery of Ireland
Bottom: A reconstruction by Stephen Conlin of the mid thirteenth-century city, looking south from the River Liffey.
Printed and bound in Poland by Białostockie Zakłady Graficzne S.A.
The paper in this book is produced using pulp from managed forests.

Published in

DUBLIN
UNESCO
City of Literature

DUBLINIA
EXPERIENCE VIKING AND MEDIEVAL DUBLIN

Funded by Dublinia, an independent,
not-for-profit organisation, dedicated
to Dublin's Viking and Medieval past.

Contents

Acknowledgements

The authors wish to thank the National Museum of Ireland and its Director, Patrick F. Wallace, for assistance with this book, in particular the photographic material pertaining to the valuable artefacts collection. Gratitude is also due to Linzi Simpson and Tim Coughlan for their kind use of photographic material. Daire O'Rourke, the first curator and education officer at Dublinia, supplied the original text on the leather-worker in chapter 6, as well as playing a crucial role in the establishment of the exhibition in its original form. Throughout that process, Anngret Simms of the Department of Geography, University College, Dublin offered invaluable advice and assistance towards the creation of an authentic portrayal of life in the medieval city.

For the intricate process of converting the present exhibition into book form, the authors are particularly indebted to Susan Houlden, whose impressive professionalism and numerous suggestions have both clarified and enlivened our presentation of the past to a general readership. In addition the authors are grateful to Donncha Ó Dúlaing, Heritage Officer, and Dublin City Council for financial support, to Suzanne Costello, Director of Dublinia, for her enthusiastic advocacy of the project, to Denise Brophy for technical advice, and to the trustees of The Medieval Trust for their sustained interest and encouragement.

The Medieval Trust is a charitable company established for educational and research purposes. Its aims include the restoration and preservation of the former Synod Hall adjoining Christ Church Cathedral and the accurate portrayal of life in medieval Dublin during the period 1170–1540. Dublinia is a project of The Medieval Trust and is intended for Dubliners and visitors alike.

Below right:
The Dublinia logo depicts two foxes dressed as pilgrims with hats, staves and satchels, a feature on a two-colour, segmental floor tile from Christ Church Cathedral. The reconstructed tiles are shown below left. A whole band of such tiles would have formed a circular arrangement, the animal pilgrims walking one behind the other in a clockwise direction. This design is believed to date from the early fourteenth century, when the satirical use of animals dressed as humans (here possibly friars begging for alms) was popular.

Preface

Ever since the Dublinia exhibition at Christ Church opened its doors to members of the public and to visitors from abroad in 1993, there has been a perceived need for a book of this kind. Many people have wished that they could take away with them a detailed and fully illustrated memento of what they had experienced. The exhibition contains a considerable amount of information about the medieval city, much of it not readily available elsewhere even to those with access to the city's libraries. Some of this material comes from records written in medieval Latin, a language that in recent times has regrettably become little known.

A core value of Dublinia has always been the accuracy and the authenticity of the historical picture that it presents to visitors, based both on surviving documents and on archaeological exploration and analysis. There is also a strong spatial dimension to the exhibition, which is represented most obviously by the scale-model of the late medieval city and by the display of post-medieval maps. Visitors to Dublinia and readers of this book with an interest in archaeology, history and historical geography should welcome this blend of the familiar and the unfamiliar, the broad generalisation and the rarefied detail, the well-known historical character and the ordinary Dubliner of past times.

The gestation of this book has been a joint venture. First, responsibility for the academic content lies with The Medieval Trust, the parent body of Dublinia Ltd. This material was gathered together for the initial version of the exhibition (1993) as well as for the subsequent refurbishment (2001). Secondly, the financial joint-sponsors are Dublin City Council and the Heritage Council; both logos are therefore reproduced side by side on the title page. The publication of such a handsomely illustrated volume would not have been possible without the practical support of these two bodies.

Introduction

Dublinia, The Story of Medieval Dublin is intended as an introduction to the city during the period 1170–1540. The text is divided into ten short chapters, each dealing with a major aspect of life in the medieval city. Background information is blended with specific details and examples.

A distinctive feature of our knowledge of Dublin in this period is the major contribution of archaeological investigations, not only at the world-famous Wood Quay site, but also at an impressive number of smaller sites. Archaeology tends to provide evidence for particular topics, e.g. dress and ornament; these are concentrated in the second half of the book. As a site is being excavated, small finds are customarily placed in a box before being taken away for analysis and conservation. We have adopted this custom as a device for containing specific archaeological information in 'finds box' sections. Readers of these chapters will thereby be in a position to compare the contribution of archaeology with that of conventional written records.

Chapter 1 includes an historical outline of the story of medieval Dublin from the Anglo-Norman takeover in 1170–2 down to the dissolution of the monasteries and hospitals *c.* 1540. Readers who like to have a rapidly absorbed overview of a new subject should find this section of value. The third chapter, on the other hand, reconstructs the city through the use of a scale-model and other illustrations. Even natives of the inner city will probably be surprised by many aspects of the model and will be intrigued by what has survived, often heavily disguised by modernity, in our own times. Chapter 7 gives particular prominence to what now constitutes a dramatic and lively initial experience in the exhibition – the ambiance of an international fair in the Middle Ages. Elaborate trading regulations are listed and the stalls include those of the baker, the scribe, the spicer, the armourer, the merchant draper and the banker. The penultimate chapter features topics relating to life and to death. A vivid impression of a typical merchant's possessions and personal values is conveyed by the inventory of the goods of Peter Higley and by his will, dating from the year 1476. He lived in the parish of St Michael the Archangel, whose church stood on the very site now occupied by Dublinia. This chapter also describes the reconstruction of a medieval face, that of a poor woman whose skeleton was found in a shallow trench on the riverward side of Christ Church Cathedral.

Opposite page: St Michael's Window at Dublinia, designed by George Walsh in 1993. The central panel shows the archangel descending towards Earth where a cooper is busy making a barrel. The fire would have been used for heating and expanding the iron bands before they were forced over the wooden staves.

Left: View of Dublinia (formerly the Synod Hall) and Christ Church Cathedral (Church of Ireland) linked by the late nineteenth-century bridge.

Above: Skull of a female skeleton discovered in the Christ Church area. The complete skeleton is currently on display at Dublinia.

Just as the story of medieval Dublin is perceived nowadays from a multidisciplinary perspective, so the authors represent the disciplines of archaeology, history and historical geography. Sarah Dent, an archaeologist by training, was the archaeological curator and education officer at Dublinia. This role had previously been performed by Ruth Johnson, who is now Dublin City Archaeologist and who has a wide-ranging involvement in all matters of archaeological concern in Dublin. Howard Clarke, who lectured in the Department of Medieval History at University College, Dublin, has a long-standing interest in topographical aspects of the medieval city and is the author of a complementary fascicle of the Royal Irish Academy's prestigious Irish Historic Towns Atlas, *Dublin, part I, to 1610* (2002). It is our collective hope that something of the excitement of the new understanding of medieval Dublin that has been achieved during the past generation will be sensed by all readers of this book.

The Time Chart

Time chart from the mid twelfth to the mid sixteenth century illustrating a selection of key events in Europe, and in Dublin in particular.

1176 Lombard League defeats Frederick I at Legnano, Italy

1179 First reference to hopped beer as an alternative to ale

Dublin 1169

ANGLO-NORMAN INVASION
Richard de Clare (Strongbow) 1170

1189 Third Crusade starts

1180 Windmill documented as an additional source of power

1170 Archbishop Thomas Becket murdered in Canterbury Cathedral, England

1187 Saladin, sultan of Egypt and Syria, captures Jerusalem

Dublin 1209

BLACK MONDAY

1194 Chartres Cathedral, France, begun in High Gothic style

1202 First Latin account of Arabic numerals

1204 Constantinople (Istanbul) sacked by crusaders

1208 Vocation of St Francis of Assisi

1212 Children's Crusade

1215 Terms of Magna Carta agreed

1233 Inquisition organized by Pope Gregory IX

1214 Philip II defeats Otto IV at Bouvines, France

Dublin 1210-28

THE BUILDING OF DUBLIN CASTLE

1241 Mongols invade central Europe

1260 First European reference to gun-powder

1260 Marco Polo arrives in Peking (Beijing), China

1282 Sicilian Vespers revolt against French rule

1291 Fall of Acre, Israel and Beirut, Lebanon

Dublin 1317

THE BRUCE INVASION: *The Burning of the Suburbs*

1306 Giotto's frescoes at Padua, Italy

1332 Moscow becomes Russian capital

Dublin 1348

THE BLACK DEATH

1347 Black Death reaches western Europe

1150   1160   1170   1180   1190   **1200**   1210   1220   1230   1240   1250   1260   1270   1280   1290   **1300**   1310   1320   1330   1340

1332   1381   1387   1431

**TIME CHART:
DUBLIN
AND THE
MEDIEVAL
WORLD**

1381
Peasants' Revolt in
England

1378
Great Schism in the
Church

1337
Hundred Years War
begins

1340
First European
papermill

1369
Hanseatic League dictates
treaty of Stralsund,
Germany

Ireland 1394-9

RICHARD II IN IRELAND:
Art MacMurrough, King of Leinster

1352
Ottoman Turks secure a
European foothold at
Gallipoli, Turkey

1387
Geoffrey Chaucer
begins to write
the Canterbury Tales

1415
Henry V defeats
French army at
Agincourt, France

1431
Joan of Arc executed at
Rouen, France

Dublin 1487

**DUBLIN AND THE WARS
OF THE ROSES:**
The Crowning of Lambert Simnel

1440
Gutenburg starts
printing by moveable
metal type

1478
Inquisition estab-
lished in Castile,
Spain

1453
Fall of
Constantinople
(Istanbul)

1488
Bartholomew Diaz
rounds Cape of Good
Hope, South Africa

1503
Leonardo da Vinci,
Mona Lisa

1492
Columbus reaches
the Bahamas,
West Indies

1507
Proposal to call
the New World
America

1529
Term
'Protestant'
first used

1535
Henry VIII assumes title
of Supreme Head of the
Church

1536
Michelangelo,
Last Judgment

1539
Surrender of the
greater monasteries
in England, Ireland
and Wales

1538
Thomas Becket's shrine at
Canterbury destroyed

Dublin 1534

**THE REBELLION OF
SILKEN THOMAS**

1517
Martin Luther posts
propositions at
Wittenberg, Germany

Dublin 1541

THE REFORMATION:
Henry VIII declared King of Ireland

1540
Europeans discover the Grand
Canyon in Arizona, America

| 1350 | 1360 | 1370 | 1380 | 1390 | **1400** | 1410 | 1420 | 1430 | 1440 | 1450 | 1460 | 1470 | 1480 | 1490 | **1500** | 1510 | 1520 | 1530 | 1540 | 1550 |

1

The Story of Medieval Dublin

Dublinia, The Story of Medieval Dublin portrays only part *of the city's long history, but it was an exciting and a formative stage with consequences that are still apparent even today.*

Ireland was never conquered by the Romans, though it was certainly influenced by their language and culture. Town life, based primarily on craftworking and on trading, dates in this country from the tenth century, when Viking Dublin became the first recognisably urban settlement on the island. By 1170 the town had an urban street pattern, defensive walls and even some tentative suburban development across the River Liffey, together with a cathedral, parish churches and monastic houses. Thereafter, with the rapid influx of colonists from abroad and from other parts of Ireland, the town grew into a city. Until *c.* 1300 Dublin participated in the great surge of urban expansion in medieval Europe, acquiring a chartered legal status amongst other things. The remainder of the period down to 1540 was largely taken up with crises brought about by political strife and by disease, and with serious economic and social problems.

The High Middle Ages

Our part of the story of medieval Dublin began over eight hundred years ago in the twelfth century, half way through the high Middle Ages, a conventional subdivision of the Middle Ages – that long period of time extending from the fall of Rome to the Italian Renaissance. The first major character was the Anglo-Norman Richard fitz Gilbert de Clare, better known as Strongbow. It was this man's thirst for power and wealth that brought him over the water from Wales to capture the rich trading town of Dublin on 21 September 1170. Ambitious to become its new ruler, Strongbow sought to establish himself by marrying Aífe, the daughter of his ally, the king of Leinster, Diarmait Mac Murchada. Diarmait died in May 1171 and soon afterwards the king of England, Henry II, paid a visit to Ireland and removed Dublin from Strongbow's grasp. Thereafter Dublin's ultimate overlord would be a foreign king in a distant land.

The population of Dublin after 1170 was a cultural mix resulting from the intermarriage of Irish, Scandinavians and the new immigrants. The number of inhabitants, estimated at 4,500 in the mid eleventh century, probably grew rapidly as craftsmen and merchants, mainly from England, joined in the colonial enterprise. Several languages were spoken in Dublin at the start of the thirteenth century. Strongbow and the ruling class would have spoken

Opposite page:
A life-sized reconstructed figure of Strongbow, the principal leader of the Anglo-Norman expedition. According to Gerald of Wales, Strongbow had reddish hair and freckles, grey eyes, a feminine face, a weak voice and a short neck, but was otherwise of tall build.

Left: The Marriage of Aífe and Strongbow by Daniel Maclise, painted in 1847. Among aristocrats, marriage was commonly used in the Middle Ages as a device for gaining political power, in this case, the kingship of Leinster. The scene is set outside the walls of Waterford.

a form of French. They were Anglo-Normans – descendants of the Normans who had invaded England in 1066 from northern France. In addition to Norman-French, a visitor to Dublin would have heard Middle English spoken by the new settlers from England, and perhaps a bit of Latin, which

Above: The top half of what has become known as Strongbow's tomb in Christ Church Cathedral. It is unlikely to be the actual monument to the Anglo-Norman knight, but a smaller and substantially older tomb displayed beside it could well be the original.

Above right: St Patrick's Cathedral (Church of Ireland), viewed from the north-east across St Patrick's Park. Part of the liberty of St Patrick, the cathedral would have been surrounded by houses and other buildings during the Middle Ages. The spire is a later addition.

was the universal language of the Church. Irish was spoken here and there but, in general, there were not many Irish people living in Dublin by that time.

For the most part the Irish were living in the surrounding countryside, over which the Anglo-Normans had only limited control. This was especially true of the district immediately to the south, in the Dublin and Wicklow Mountains. On Easter Monday 1209, the citizens of Dublin ventured outside the safety of the city walls to a spot known as Cullenswood (now Ranelagh). A group of Irish warriors from the mountains fell upon them and massacred about five hundred people. In memory of this event, the day came to be known as Black Monday. The walls themselves dated back to the late Viking Age *c.* 1100, but by this time the newcomers had made some improvements. For example, Newgate is described as 'the new west gate' of Dublin in 1177, the year following Strongbow's death and his burial in Christ Church Cathedral. His tomb, incidentally, became a place of veneration for the rest of the Middle Ages; it was, however, virtually destroyed when the nave roof and the south wall collapsed in 1562 and only a broken remnant now survives.

In the early thirteenth century the archbishop of Dublin, Henry Blund 'de Londres' (1213–28), began the building of Dublin Castle on the site of an earlier one – a project that started *c.* 1210 and took about twenty years to complete, using simple plans. The castle was built to withstand attack in case of war and to be a symbol of Archbishop Henry's political power as justiciar or governor of Ireland. King John gave him the title of justiciar, hoping to use him to maintain power over the unruly Anglo-Norman knights, who might otherwise see Dublin as a power-base for challenges to the English crown. It was during Archbishop Henry's time that the existing suburban church of St Patrick was raised to cathedral status *c.* 1220, thereby creating a second 'chapter' to rival that of Christ Church, the older cathedral in the heart of the walled city.

The Late Middle Ages

A hundred years after the building of Dublin Castle, in 1317, the city was in danger of imminent attack by a massive army led by the Scotsman, Edward the Bruce, and his brother, King Robert. Edward was determined to take Dublin for his own as part of a wider plan to help his brother to expel the English from Scotland. By February, Edward's army was camped only 8 kilometres (approximately 5 miles) away from the city, forcing the mayor to take drastic action. He ordered that the suburbs beyond the city walls should be burnt in preparation for what was expected to be a damaging and protracted siege. Although the mayor's plan ultimately worked and prevented Edward's attack, the flames got out of control and much more of Dublin was burnt than had been intended.

The Black Death was the greatest catastrophe in recorded human history. Victims would have been confined to their homes, their doors marked with a symbol indicating the presence of disease.

In August 1348, shortly after it reached England, the Black Death came to Dublin. The disease was carried there aboard trading ships by black rats and was probably transmitted to humans by bites from fleas. Once a person contracted bubonic plague, parts of their body would break out in black boils. Although the victims might have had only a few days to live, there was still some chance of survival. It was not long, however, before more deadly strains of the disease developed. The plague spread rapidly in the crowded streets and lanes of Dublin and victims could die within a matter of hours. These strains are still some of the deadliest diseases known in the history of mankind. The whole city fell victim to this sickness and, at night, carts brought hundreds of corpses to mass graves in the part of Dublin known as the Black Pitts, in the southern suburb just west of modern New Street. As a result, the city's population may have fallen dramatically from a peak of about 11,000 in the late thirteenth century to only half that number by *c.* 1400.

Despite the enormity of the epidemic, and the fact that plague returned to Dublin from time to time afterwards, the survivors were able to adapt to their circumstances and to look forward to new opportunities. As the suburbs were depopulated, some of the inhabitants may have been able to obtain better housing within the security of the walls. A collection of wills and inventories of goods dating from the third quarter of the fifteenth century indicates that the upper and middling social levels of the city and its immediate surroundings enjoyed a reasonable degree of personal comfort in their homes by contemporary standards.

With Dublin weakened, it was inevitable that ambitious people would take advantage of the situation. One of the Irish kings who gave the English trouble was Art Mór Mac Murchadha, king of Leinster (1375–1416) and a descendant of the same family that Strongbow had married into two hundred years before. All along, when the Anglo-Normans were colonising and developing Dublin and other towns, bringing them under the control of the English crown, the Irish were successful in keeping their own royal courts, their style of dress and their language, and they continued to rule

Above: Art Mór Mac Murchadha, king of Leinster, shown in the company of his dog, an Irish wolfhound. Despite his warrior-like appearance, the presence of books symbolises the standard of literacy of some late medieval Irish kings.

Right: A scene depicting a meeting between English forces and the Leinster Irish, painted by a French artist. The Irish warriors are shown emerging from heavily wooded mountains and the two parties are separated by a stream.

much of the island. Moreover, by the end of the fourteenth century, four of the Irish kings, including Mac Murchadha, had become so powerful as to make King Richard II distinctly unsure of his hold over Ireland. Richard decided to pay a visit to Ireland in 1394 and it is believed that he received each of the Irish kings in Christ Church Cathedral and made them swear allegiance to him.

Almost a hundred years later, in 1487, King Henry VII – Henry Tudor – was on the English throne, despite the fact that he had no legitimate claim to it in the male line, being descended from a minor landowning family in North Wales. His position was unstable and his enemies were looking for an opportunity to overthrow him. Their chance came in the form of a ten-year-old boy called Lambert Simnel, who was taken to Christ Church Cathedral and crowned King Edward VI of England, making him a pretender to the throne. The story goes that once Lambert Simnel had been crowned, he was put on the shoulders of the tallest man around – a certain Sir William D'Arcy – and paraded through the city streets in the company of the archbishop, the mayor, a large gathering of other dignitaries and 2,000 foreign mercenaries hired to protect the boy king.

Despite the pomp and ceremony, however, the plot ended in failure when Lambert Simnel was taken, with an army, over to England. The army was defeated, the boy captured, and Henry VII took great delight in having the youth – his former rival to the throne – serve him and his guests at table as a common servant. Simnel's ultimate fate is unknown. A key figure behind this plot was the earl of Kildare, Gearóid Mór Fitzgerald (1478–1513), by now

Left: The crown worn by the young Lambert is reported to have been taken from a statue of the Virgin Mary in the church of St Mary del Dam. The parish of this church consisted of little more than Dublin Castle.

Right: Stephen Conlin's painting of an expanding city shows the castle at an advanced stage of construction and Christ Church Cathedral before the nave was completed. Newly reclaimed land from the river at Wood Quay is shown in the foreground.

one of the most powerful men in Ireland and a potential enemy of the king of England. His great castle at Maynooth enabled him to influence events in Dublin, of which he had become a freeman in 1478. Parts of the present ruins at the main entrance to National University of Ireland, Maynooth, date back to his time.

The Beginning of Modern Times

In 1534 Gearóid Mór's grandson and deputy governor of Anglo-Ireland, Lord Thomas Fitzgerald, was to offer the next Irish challenge to English rule. Fitzgerald, who was known to the people as Silken Thomas because of his love of finery, heard false news that King Henry VIII had executed his father. Fearful for his family's safety and position, and in a passionate fury, Silken Thomas raised an army and marched on Dublin, storming into the chapter-house (which still survives) of St Mary's Abbey where the king's council was having a secret meeting. He slammed down the great Sword of State on to the table, publicly resigned his office and declared himself a sworn enemy of the king. Silken Thomas and his army then besieged the king's castle and the city's Newgate in an attempt to kill or to expel Henry VIII's men, but they were eventually defeated. The young lord was taken to England and later executed for his treachery.

The early sixteenth century was a turbulent period and Henry VIII's break with the church of Rome brought more trouble to Dublin. In denying

Chapter-house of St Mary's Abbey, looking east. St Mary's was one of the largest and most important monasteries in Ireland until its suppression in the sixteenth century. Chapter-houses were sometimes used for meetings by people other than the monks themselves.

Table of Kings of England and Overlords of Dublin

Plantagenet Rulers

Henry II	1154–89
(overlord from 1171)	
Richard I	1189–99
John	1199–1216
Henry III	1216–72
Edward I	1272–1307
Edward II	1307–27
Edward III	1327–77
Richard II	1377–99

Lancastrian Rulers

Henry IV	1399–1413
Henry V	1413–22
Henry VI	1422–61, 1470–1

Yorkist Rulers

Edward IV	1461–70, 1471–83
Edward V	1483
Richard III	1483–5

Tudor Rulers

Henry VII	1485–1509
Henry VIII	1509–47
(also king of Ireland from 1541)	

the authority of the pope in Rome, King Henry not only gained political power over the church in England, but also saw the chance to obtain some of its immense wealth. He plundered and broke up the religious institutions of England and Ireland that remained loyal to the pope. The new archbishop of Dublin, George Browne (1536–54), brought English troops to Ireland and ordered that relics such as the Bacall Íosa (Staff of Jesus) in Christ Church Cathedral be taken and burnt in the streets outside. During this period, many other priceless relics that were sacred to the Irish and the Anglo-Irish were destroyed or dispersed.

The enforced closure of the monasteries brought about a revolution in landholding in the city. All but one of the religious houses – Holy Trinity Priory, attached to Christ Church Cathedral

Portrait of Henry VIII (detail) by Hans Holbein, *c.* 1536–7. Intended to commemorate the strengths and triumphs of the Tudor dynasty, this preparatory drawing in its entirety also showed the king's parents and his third wife, Jane Seymour.

– were situated in the suburbs and it was there that opportunities arose for church property to be taken over by laymen. Most of the monastic churches themselves were plundered and demolished, though ancillary buildings of good quality could be used for other purposes. The most durable of these changes was the adaptation of the site of All Saints' Priory to the requirements of a university in the 1590s, marking the beginning of the long and distinguished history of Trinity College. These physical changes of the sixteenth century started the process whereby the medieval city was largely destroyed. A new epoch in recorded history was being born – that which we still call 'modern'.

2

The Colony

Starting off as two Gaelic settlements, Dublin evolved in the tenth century into a Viking town that became a great international trading centre; after 1170 it expanded into an Anglo-Norman city and the chief administrative centre of that part of Ireland which was under colonial control.

Medieval Europe was characterised by powerful forces for expansion and contraction; the settlement of Dublin was formed under the influence of a whole succession of these. As a place of permanent habitation, it was established by the Irish long before the Vikings arrived. The latter took over the existing settlements and developed a trading colony far removed from their homelands. These two peoples – the Irish and the Scandinavians – having fused into a mixed cultural group called by modern scholars Hiberno-Norse, were themselves supplanted by the even more dynamic Anglo-Normans. They colonised Ireland more extensively than their predecessors, before being reduced by the end of the Middle Ages to the area that came to be known as the Pale. The medieval colony barely survived, but in the post-Reformation period the Pale, including Dublin, became the basis of a more thorough, and more ruthless, conquest of the whole island.

What's in a Name?

'Dublin' is the English and international name of the city, but it is not the oldest name. The original settlement, going back to prehistoric times, was called Áth Cliath and the official modern name in Irish is derived from this – Baile Átha Cliath. The two names are clearly quite different, which tells us something important about the origins of Dublin.

Áth Cliath ('ford of hurdle-work') took its name from a major ford, first documented in the sixth century AD, across the tidal River Liffey. The precise location of this ford has not yet been established, but was probably a short distance upstream from present-day Father Mathew Bridge. The hurdles

Opposite page: Detail of Stephen Conlin's painting of Dublin Castle, showing the north-eastern angle-tower known as the Powder Tower. Originally five storeys high, its sloping base still survives underground and can be seen by visitors today.

This page: A section of a scale-model of Dublin, *c.* 1500, showing Christ Church Cathedral in the centre. The reclaimed area of the thirteenth century at Wood Quay and Merchant's Quay extends between the semi-ruinous inner north wall and the later riverside wall.

are presumed to have been wattle screens forming permanent rafts that enabled people and animals to walk on the exposed mud-flats at low tide. The early settlement grew up in the Cornmarket area on top of a low east-west ridge overlooking the river crossing. This ridgeway would later become the main axis of the medieval city and is now represented by Castle Street, Christchurch Place, High Street, Cornmarket and Thomas Street.

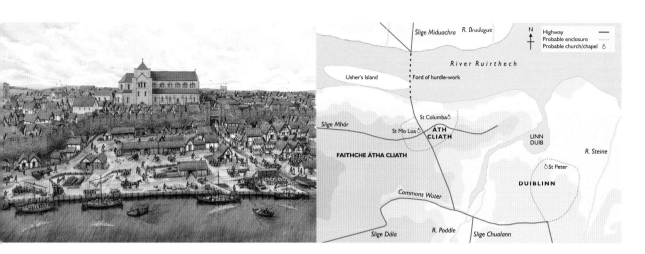

Map labels: Slige Miduachra, R. Brudugue, River Ruirtech, Highway, Probable enclosure, Probable church/chapel, Usher's Island, Ford of hurdle-work, St Columba, Slige Mhór, St Mo Lua, ÁTH CLIATH, LINN DUIB, R. Steine, FAITHCHE ÁTHA CLIATH, St Peter, DUIBLINN, Commons Water, Slige Dála, R. Poddle, Slige Chualann

Above left: A reconstruction by Stephen Conlin of the mid thirteenth-century city, looking south from the River Liffey. It shows the inner north wall with King's Gate and Christ Church Cathedral near the summit of the ridge.

Above right: Map of Dublin, *c.* 840, showing the wide River Ruirthech (Liffey) flowing into the nearby bay. Two settlements are shown: the earlier, Áth Cliath, on the east-west ridge, and the later, Duiblinn, south of the tidal pool in the Poddle.

Right: Map of Ireland *c.* 1540. Dublin is represented on the map in accordance with the conventions of this period. The number of symbolic buildings indicates that it was one of the largest settlements on the island. Leinster appears as *Lagenia*.

Probably in the sixth century a monastery was founded due south of a tidal pool in the River Poddle, a tributary of the Liffey. The depth of the water in this pool would have varied with the ebb and flow of the tide, but it could have accommodated the shallow-draughted vessels of those times. Its name was Duiblinn ('black pool', modernised as Dubhlinn) and its site has never been built over; today it is easily recognisable as the roughly circular garden behind Dublin Castle. A characteristic feature of Irish monastic sites – an oval-shaped enclosure – is still partly preserved in the street pattern near the site of the pool in the Aungier Street area, the streets in question being Peter Row, Whitefriar Street, Upper and Lower Stephen Street, and Johnson Place.

Later on, the bay and the pool attracted the Vikings, who came from both Norway and Denmark and who needed to protect their ships from seaward storms and from landward attacks. Having settled nearby, they corrupted the Gaelic name into Dyflinn, which is the form found in Icelandic sources recording traditions associated with the Vikings. The territorial kingdom was known to the Norsemen as Dyflinnarskíri (Dublinshire).

To judge from Latin documents after 1170 the Anglo-Normans continued this

process of changing the name, as speakers of French and writers of Latin. Several Latin versions of the place-name are recorded, but one of the commonest is Dublinia, as shown on the accompanying map.

A Town in the Making

Dublin had long been a town when it was captured by the king of Leinster, Diarmait Mac Murchada, and by his Anglo-Norman allies in 1170. The latter were led by Richard fitz Gilbert de Clare, nicknamed Strongbow. The town's origins were both Gaelic and Scandinavian, with the result that the inhabitants of the eleventh and twelfth centuries were culturally mixed. Hiberno-Norse Dublin appears to have had a thriving economy through widespread international trading contacts with Scandinavia, Iceland, Britain and, later, with northern France.

The location of Dublin as a settlement was determined in the mists of time by the need for a safe passage across the River Liffey. Before the arrival of the Vikings in the ninth century there were *two* important settlement sites south of the Liffey – secular Áth Cliath and monastic Dubhlinn.

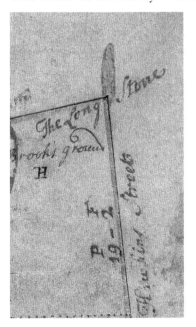

Survivals of early monastic life in and around Dublin include the Finglas high cross and the shaft of another high cross at Kilmainham. Relatively plain crosses such as these would have helped to demarcate the sacred space afforded by the enclosure and to denote the sanctuary offered to everyone inside it – monks, nuns, their relatives, local lords (including kings), monastic tenants, pilgrims and other visitors.

The Vikings commemorated their first landfall at this strategic spot by erecting a large standing stone on the margin of Dublin Bay. Known as the Long Stone, it survived down to the eighteenth century

Below: Finglas high cross. The monastery at Finglas, along with that at Tallaght, was particularly important in the late eighth century as a centre of the church reform movement in Ireland known as the Céli Dé.

Below left: Eighteenth-century map showing the Viking Long Stone. Streets such as Hawkins Street, which are named on the map, enable us to pinpoint the exact location of the Long Stone. It may have stood up to 4 metres high (13 feet).

and its precise position is recorded on a map of 1718. A modern replica at the southern end of D'Olier Street marks more or less the exact spot.

In the course of the tenth century a recognisable town developed at the eastern end of the ridge, at the point where the River Poddle entered the Liffey. A good deal of archaeological evidence has been recovered from the district north and south of Lord Edward Street (a much later thoroughfare). By 1170 this town had a stone enclosing wall, Christ Church Cathedral and a number of other churches, three extramural monasteries of recent foundation, and a suburb across the bridge on the northern bank, which later acquired the name Oxmantown. Parts of the early town wall have been found in excavations at Wood Quay, Ross Road (linking Patrick Street and Bride Street), and at the foundation level of the Powder Tower of Dublin Castle.

The conversion of the pagan Vikings to Christianity seems to have occurred over a long period of time and may have owed much to their Irish – presumably Christian – wives, concubines and female slaves. A distinctive artefact from the Hiberno-Norse period (*c.* 980 to *c.* 1170) is a particular type of grave-slab belonging to the so-called Rathdown group. Six of these survived to be incorporated into the fabric of St Patrick's Cathedral when it was being built during the second quarter of the thirteenth century. Another example may be seen in the vestibule of St Audoen's Church (Church of Ireland) in Cornmarket.

Drawing of an early grave-slab from St Patrick's Cathedral, showing two high crosses. Its preservation in the thirteenth-century cathedral implies that it was taken from a much earlier burial ground on the same site.

The death of King Harold II as shown on the Bayeux Tapestry. A figure labelled as Harold, attempting to remove an arrow from his eye, is followed by another figure being struck down by a mounted Norman knight. Both could represent the king.

24

The Hiberno-Norse town was captured in 1170 by people who are traditionally called 'Normans'. Personal names such as Richard fitz Gilbert de Clare, Miles de Cogan and Raymond le Gros ('the fat') are expressive of their continental origins in a French-speaking milieu. These descendants of Viking settlers in northern France had earlier defeated the Anglo-Danish king of England, Harold II, at the famous battle of Hastings in 1066 under the leadership of William the Conqueror. His ruling dynasty had in turn been undermined by the civil war that took place in England and Normandy during the reign of Stephen (1135–54). The victorious side came to be represented by Henry, the son of the count of Anjou whose mother was Anglo-Norman. As King Henry II of England he came to Ireland in the winter of 1171–2 and spent most of his time at Dublin.

Portrait of King Stephen with his pet falcon. Hunting with falcons was a common aristocratic pastime in the Middle Ages, and these valuable birds were sometimes presented as gifts.

A Colonial Capital

Anglo-Norman Dublin was an administrative centre in two different ways. Besides its role as a self-governing municipality, it was for most of our period the governmental headquarters of the lordship of Ireland. Though not a capital city in the modern sense of a permanent seat of central government, Dublin was by far the most important town in medieval Ireland and its castle was the biggest royal stronghold in the colony.

The castle was sited in the south-eastern angle of the existing Hiberno-Norse walls, where the waters of the Poddle had the potential to feed its

Painting of Dublin Castle in the late fifteenth century looking south, by Stephen Conlin. The courtyard is depicted full of activity as foot soldiers are marshalled and stores are unloaded. Part of the former moat is shown being cultivated as a garden.

Below left: A section of a scale-model of Dublin, *c.* 1500, showing Dublin Castle. The River Poddle still gave protection to the castle on the east and south sides, but the moat was no longer water-filled by this date.

Below right: Dublin Castle viewed from the south-west, showing the modern garden on the site of the earlier tidal pool. The only surviving angle-tower, called the Record Tower, is clearly visible with its elaborate battlements added in the nineteenth century.

moat. The first castle was probably built hastily of earth and timber, in order to protect the garrison of forty knights left behind by Henry II early in 1172. Its gate is documented before Strongbow's death four years later; other recorded details are a bridge, a prison and a kitchen.

A stronger, stone castle was commissioned by King John in 1204. Initially a traditional square keep may have been envisaged, but keeps were going out of fashion around the turn of the twelfth century. Instead a powerful, roughly rectangular walled enclosure with angle-towers at each corner and an elaborate gatehouse and turnbridge in the middle of the northern side, facing the city, were built. The interior of the courtyard, corresponding to the present Upper Yard, was occupied by domestic buildings of various kinds, especially the King's Hall measuring 120 by 80 (medieval) feet. Building timber was brought in from the Wicklow area, possibly from the royal forest at Glencree.

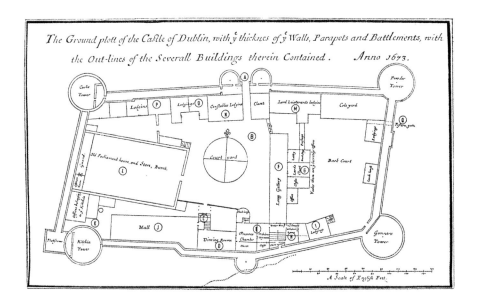

The Ground plott of the Castle of Dublin, with $\check{y}$ thickness of $\check{y}$ Walls, Parapets and Battlements, with the Out-lines of the Severall Buildings therein Contained. Anno 1673.

Above left: Plan of Dublin Castle, dated 1673. It was the last and most detailed to be made before the fire of 1684. The former King's Hall and many other administrative buildings are ranged around the main courtyard.

Above right: The archway over the north ditch, which formerly gave access to that side of the castle by boat from the River Poddle. It was closed up during the late fourteenth or fifteenth century. The upper arch is known as a relieving arch.

Below: King Henry II and Queen Eleanor crossing the English Channel. Henry II's 'empire' included the vast duchy of Aquitaine in south-western France, which he acquired by marrying the feisty and flirtatious Eleanor, the divorced queen of the French king, in 1152.

On the northern and western sides of Dublin Castle an impressive, U-shaped moat, partly rock-cut, measured approximately 22 metres (72 feet) wide and 10 metres (33 feet) deep. An archway over the east end of the north ditch gave access to small boats using the River Poddle; this can still be viewed deep underground by visitors to the Powder Tower. Some other medieval castles, for instance the Tower of London, had a more sophisticated watergate serving a similar purpose.

The lordship of Ireland was created in 1177 by King Henry II for his youngest son, John, and it lasted until Henry VIII assumed the title of king of Ireland in 1541. The king's chief representative in Ireland was usually called the justiciar until the late fourteenth century and was subsequently called the lieutenant or deputy to the lieutenant. He would travel around the colony with his administrative assistants, but he had special quarters in Dublin Castle as well.

For most of the period 1170–1540 the exchequer, or financial headquarters, was located at Dublin. In the early days of the colony the buildings stood outside

the walls near modern Exchequer Street; later on, as conditions grew more insecure, rented houses inside the walls and parts of the castle were used instead. The exchequer takes its name from a large chequered cloth covering the table around which officials and sheriffs sat. The squares were used for making and demonstrating calculations for the benefit of those who were illiterate. A drawing (now destroyed) was made of the Irish exchequer in the fifteenth century.

Above: William of Windsor, lieutenant of Ireland, 1369–72, was vigorous in trying to bring order to that part of Ireland which was under colonial rule. His forceful attempts to raise funds and troops, including from Dublin, met with loud resistance and he was removed from office.

Right: Late medieval drawing of the Irish exchequer, showing the chequered cloth in the centre, along with counters and some coins. The principal officers and clerks sit around three sides and a sheriff, settling his account, sits facing them in the foreground.

The Pale

The Pale was the main block of territory in late medieval Ireland that was still theoretically loyal to the English crown. First documented in the late fifteenth century, it came to be demarcated by the course of a river or elsewhere by an earthen bank and ditch. Beyond the Pale lay the mysterious and, to the Dublin residents, hostile world of the Irish, who had succeeded in recovering control of most of the island. This was despite the fact that, during the fourteenth and fifteenth centuries, English colonial administrators had organised numerous military expeditions both east and west of the Dublin and Wicklow Mountains. The recently discovered fort at Carrickmines may have functioned as a forward-base for expeditions of this kind.

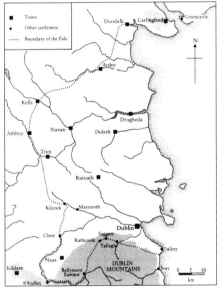

The massacre of several hundred citizens at Cullenswood (Ranelagh) on Easter Monday 1209 (recorded in the sixteenth century and commemorated as Black Monday) pinpointed the exposure of the colonists to attack from the mountains to the south of Dublin. But in practice the city developed very extensive suburbs during the thirteenth century and it is not until the fifteenth century that there are consistent reports of a renewed sense of vulnerability. At this time a large number of tower-houses were built, church towers took on a fortified appearance, the Pale was defined by an act of the Irish parliament in 1488, and six years later another act provided for the construction of a double embankment 2 metres (6 feet) high. A good example of such a tower-house still survives as Dundrum Castle, in a modern

Left: A drawing of attendants of Irish soldiers (towards the right) by Albrecht Dürer, made on the Continent in 1521. Two distinctive features of Irish fashion for men are the glib, a large lock of hair falling over the forehead, and the moustache.

Right: Map showing the approximate extent of the Pale, corresponding to the historic County Dublin and much of Counties Kildare, Louth and Meath. These were known as the four 'obedient' shires in the fifteenth century before the Pale was formally created.

Right: The west tower of Balrothery Church, County Fingal. Balrothery lies a short distance south of Balbriggan. The tower has some of the properties of a tower-house, and may also have served as the parish priest's residence.

Below left: View of Genevel's Tower/Genevel's Inns at Ross Road, as excavated by Claire Walsh. Both the mural tower and the residence date from the early thirteenth century.

Above right: End-panel of the St Lawrence tomb in St Mary's Church, Howth. Dating from c. 1470, the panel shows (from left to right) an unidentified saint, St Thomas of Canterbury, St Katherine of Alexandria (notice her wheel), and St Peter with his key.

suburb that in those days would have been a vulnerable colonial outpost only a short distance from the threatening mountains.

The Pale had little military significance; its main practical purposes were to protect arable land and to prevent cattle from being stolen and driven away. Such a boundary was also a political statement, proclaiming the area where the king's writ was still obeyed in what was referred to as the land of peace. Peaceful conditions were an important consideration for merchants and the Pale may have played a part in ensuring that Dublin and Drogheda in particular could continue to function as successful ports, trading both with their hinterlands and with the outside world.

3

A City Reconstructed

The scale-model of Dublin shows how the walled city
and its impressive suburbs extending in all directions would have
looked towards the end of the Middle Ages.

The illustrations in this chapter show an overview, and sections, of a 1:300 scale-model of the greater part of Dublin as it would have appeared towards the end of the Middle Ages *c.* 1500. One of the most striking features is the small size of the walled area – about 18 hectares (44 acres) – as compared with the relatively undefended suburbs. The suburbs were protected to some degree by extramural gateways controlling access along the main approach roads; many of these date probably from the fifteenth century, when the much-reduced colonial territory known as the Pale was being established both as a concept and as a boundary. Altogether about twenty extramural gates are documented. A good example stood where Thomas Street gives way to James's Street; a later age would see the construction on adjacent ground of St James's Gate Brewery – the original home of Guinness.

The Course of the City Walls

Taking Dublin Castle as a starting-point, the south wall ran along Little Ship Street, where it can still be seen together with a mural tower called Stanihurst's Tower. In the Middle Ages this tower was round rather than angular on the outside. The two openings giving access to the southern suburb were Pool Gate and St Nicholas's Gate, named respectively after the

Above left: Close-up of the western city wall at Lamb Alley. The wall is roughly coursed and made of calp limestone. This dark-grey mottled stone formed the bedrock under the city and was quarried extensively for stone buildings.

Above right: Inner face of the Hiberno-Norse wall at Wood Quay. In 1980 workers numbered the stones before large sections of Ireland's oldest town wall were dismantled. Part of the wall was retained underneath the Civic Offices.

tidal pool in the Poddle and a parish church inside the walls. Outside the wall St Nicholas's Street became St Patrick's Street, heading southwards past the great cathedral.

The line of the western wall is followed nowadays by Lamb Alley, where a smaller and somewhat forlorn piece of stonework still stands in the shadow of a modern building. This piece of wall has been conserved by Dublin City Council. Having no natural water defences, the west wall was paralleled externally by the city ditch, which was up to 40 medieval feet wide and 19 feet deep (it is not known whether medieval feet were smaller or larger than modern-day feet). Again two gates gave access to this suburb: Newgate facing Thomas Street and Gormond's Gate facing Crockers' Lane or Street (now Mullinahack and Oliver Bond Street).

On the north side, towards the River Liffey, there were two lines of defence. The older, inner wall was first built *c.* 1100 and subsequently modified by the Anglo-Normans in the thirteenth century. A fine stretch can still be

seen in Cook Street, together with the only surviving city gateway, St Audoen's Arch. Outside this wall, the area of reclaimed land was initially defended towards the east and west; here a surviving remnant represents the lowest courses of Isolde's Tower in Lower Exchange Street, conserved and visible to the public below ground level. Access to the main bridge and the northside suburb of Oxmantown was via Bridge Gate.

Finally, towards the east, the city wall ran behind Upper Exchange Street and back to the castle. The eastern suburb extended outside Dam Gate, so called after the dam across the River Poddle that kept its waters deep enough to feed the castle's great moat. The nearby parish church of St Mary del Dam, where City Hall now stands, recalls the same feature, as does modern Dame Street.

Using the scale-model as a guide to the imagination, we shall now create an impression of approaching the city from different directions towards the end of the Middle Ages.

Left: St Audoen's Arch. The arch dates from the early thirteenth century, but has since been modified. It was one of a number of gates designed to link the old city with the land reclaimed from the River Liffey.

Right: The tower of St Audoen's Church (Church of Ireland), largely rebuilt in the seventeenth century, is out of alignment with the thirteenth-century nave. Immediately behind stands the massive nineteenth-century Roman Catholic church.

The Eastern Approach from Dublin Bay

A late medieval visitor to Dublin coming from abroad would have sailed up the tidal estuary of the River Liffey before most of the quays had been built. On the left the old Viking assembly place (the Thingmount, now the site of the Ulster Bank and adjoining buildings on Suffolk Street) and its associated

33

Scale-model of Dublin,
c. 1500, viewed from the
south with St Patrick's
Cathedral in the
foreground. The central
part of the model is
shown, including the
entire walled city and
parts of all four suburbs

1. Augustinian friary of Holy Trinity
2. Dam Mills
3. King's Hall
4. Isolde's Tower
5. Merchant's Quay
6. Wood Quay
7. Christ Church Cathedral
8. St Patrick's Cathedral
9. St Sepulchre's Palace
10. St Peter's Church
11. Carmelite monastery
12. Franciscan friary
13. Fair Green
14. Newgate
15. St John the Baptist's Hospital
16. St Audoen's Church
17. St Saviour's Priory
18. Chapel
19. St Audoen's Arch
20. St Michael the Archangel's Church

(See also references on pp36–43)

burial-mounds would have come into view. The name of this public open space, Hoggen Green (now College Green) was probably derived from the Old Norse word *haugar,* meaning 'burial-mounds'. One of these burials, apparently very elaborate, still survived in the 1640s, when it was described and drawn. A small number of Viking artefacts from the vicinity have been preserved. The Thingmount itself was demolished in 1685 and its soil used to raise the level of St Patrick's Well Lane (now Nassau Street) in order to prevent flooding.

Right: Precinct wall of Holy Trinity Friary at Cecilia Street, Temple Bar, as excavated by Linzi Simpson. This section was rebuilt and is now within the basement of a restaurant. The triangular keystone of this relieving arch can be seen at the apex.

Below: A quern or stone handmill. In addition to water mills, rotary quern stones were used to grind corn by hand. The grain was funnelled through the hole in the upper stone, which would have been turned by means of a wooden handle.

Three monasteries could also have been seen by our late medieval visitor: the nunnery of St Mary de Hogges, founded by Diarmait Mac Murchada *c.* 1146 (near the new Dublin Tourism Centre), the Augustinian monastery of All Saints (or All Hallows), also founded by Diarmait Mac Murchada, and the Augustinian friary of Holy Trinity, founded some time before 1282 (in present-day Temple Bar) (**1**). At the mouth of the Poddle, Dam Mills were grinding corn for the inhabitants (**2**); many other mills were needed for this purpose. Just beyond the eastern gateway into the city, parts of Dublin Castle, the biggest royal stronghold in medieval Ireland, could have been seen. Its main courtyard was encompassed by powerful angle-towers and high curtain walls, inside which were several

other buildings. These included the King's Hall (3) where parliaments were sometimes held.

At the north-eastern corner of the defences beside the Liffey stood a circular tower named either after a local landowner or after the popular fictional character, Isolde (4). If the former is the true derivation of the name, it illustrates the fact that women could be significant property-owners in medieval times; in the alternative interpretation, it reflects the diffusion of an early thirteenth-century German literary work, *Tristan and Isolde*, celebrating romantic as distinct from chivalric love, along the trade routes of Europe to Ireland. Merchants and travellers in the late Middle Ages landed at Merchant's Quay (5) or Wood Quay (6). Behind these quays the city rose up dramatically on its natural ridge, with Christ Church Cathedral (7) in the centre. At the nearby main crossroads stood the High Cross, which is first documented in 1326. As today, the medieval city would have been clearly visible from the Dublin Mountains, though of course it was very much smaller in extent. The Irish inhabitants of the mountains are known to have traded, as well as raided, in the southern suburb of the city.

Isolde's Tower was built in the mid thirteenth century to protect the north-east angle of the city wall, which projected into the River Liffey. The defensive calp limestone walls (preserved under a modern apartment building in Lower Exchange Street) are a massive 3.9 metres (13 feet) thick.

37

The Southern Approach from Harold's Cross and Rathfarnham

From the south the most dramatic feature was the biggest church in medieval Ireland, St Patrick's Cathedral (**8**), established as a cathedral *c.* 1220 and standing inside its own enclosure fortified by walls and tower-houses. These protected the numerous important buildings associated with the life of a great cathedral, including the archbishop's palace known as St

The choir of St Patrick's Cathedral, looking east. Built in the second quarter of the thirteenth century, the elegant proportions of the Gothic arcades and windows are particularly striking. The choir stalls are of later date.

Sepulchre's (until recently Kevin Street garda station) (**9**). This palace was the administrative centre of a large 'manor' or estate that extended southwards for some distance. Some of the medieval archbishops resided there, but a survey of the year 1326 shows that the buildings were in poor condition: the stone hall roofed with shingles (wooden tiles), chamber, kitchen and chapel are all described as being 'of no value and in disrepair'. Some late medieval archbishops preferred to live in the more salubrious rural surroundings of Swords or Tallaght, where they had other estates.

No other town or city in Latin Christendom had two cathedrals juxtaposed like Christ Church and St Patrick's. Constitutionally the archbishops' two cathedrals were run on quite different lines, Christ Church by its Augustinian monks under their prior, and St Patrick's by its secular canons under their dean. Both models had been imported from England, whose cathedrals in the Middle Ages were divided roughly half-and-half on a similar basis. For nearly a century (*c.* 1228 to *c.* 1317) there was a good deal of friction between the competing chapters or governing bodies, until the papacy took a more proactive part in 'providing' (nominating) senior churchmen.

To the east of the cathedral complex was the much older, oval-shaped ecclesiastical enclosure representing the early medieval monastery at Dubhlinn (now traversed by Aungier Street). By the end of the Middle Ages this ancient site was occupied by the parish church of St Peter (**10**), a Carmelite monastery (on a site that was reclaimed by the same religious order in the nineteenth century) (**11**), and the leper hospital of St Stephen (now Mercer Court and Mercer Library). St Stephen's in turn gave its name

Left: Painting of St Patrick's Cathedral from the north, *c.* 1500, by Stephen Conlin. The cathedral is shown surrounded by half-timbered buildings and without the spire, which was added in the mid eighteenth century. St Sepulchre's Palace can be seen to the left of the cathedral.

Right: A section of the scale-model, showing the southern suburb of the city from the south. In the foreground, St Patrick's Cathedral and St Sepulchre's Palace are visible and the Franciscan friary in Francis Street can be seen in the distance towards the left. The main walled city forms the backdrop.

39

to the extensive public space that is still known as St Stephen's Green and was then a common pasture for animals belonging to the citizens. Only a small part of the green is shown on the model, together with the southern end of the laneway that is the ancestor of Grafton Street. North-west of St Patrick's stood the Franciscan friary (now St Nicholas of Myra's Church) (**12**), founded by Henry III before 1233 and after which Francis Street was named. Heading off in a westerly direction along The Coombe (meaning 'valley') was an ancient routeway, which followed the course of a small stream.

The Western Approach from Kilmainham and Chapelizod

A traveller from the interior of Ireland would have passed along a major suburban thoroughfare, which was also very ancient, Thomas Street. This street was named after the great Augustinian abbey dedicated to St Thomas Becket, founded initially as a priory by Henry II in 1177. Becket had been assassinated inside his own cathedral at Canterbury in December 1170 by four knights, allegedly encouraged to do so by an exasperated king after several years of wrangling with his former friend. The main subject of dispute had been the trial of 'criminous clerks' (priests and men in lesser orders who had committed crimes). The murder caused grave scandal throughout Latin Christendom and the king was forced to perform various acts of penance in its aftermath.

In front of St Thomas's stood the parish church of St Catherine, an early thirteenth-century foundation. Before reaching the abbey's precinct on the southern side of the street the late medieval visitor would have passed through St James's Gate (too far outside the city to be shown on the model), one of many extramural gates that helped to provide security in the early days of the Pale. Along the northern side of the street flowed the citizens' main fresh water supply, which was routed by means of a series of artificial channels that carried the combined waters of the Poddle and the Dodder.

Only this western side of the walled city lacked a watercourse as a means of protection, hence the construction of the great ditch. Fairs were held

The mid fourteenth-century chancel and south aisle were built as major extensions to St Audoen's, whose nave (far left) is the only surviving remnant of a parish church from the Middle Ages still in use in Dublin.

each summer on the green space in front of the ditch (**13**). The centrepiece of the western wall was Newgate (at the west end of Cornmarket) (**14**), whose right-hand tower contained the city prison. Outside this gate stood the hospital of St John the Baptist (now St John the Baptist and St Augustine's Church), a home for sick poor people founded very soon after the coming of the Anglo-Normans (**15**). Inside the gate lay a market space and beyond that High Street followed the crest of the ridge, where meat was sold and where leather-workers were based. Medieval Dublin had no regular, planned market place of the kind that is commonly found in towns on the Continent. On the northern side of Cornmarket stood St Audoen's Church (**16**), the biggest parish church south of the Liffey, parts of which survive today as a place of worship and as a visitor centre. Its dedication to a French saint (St Ouen, of Rouen in Normandy) suggests an Anglo-Norman foundation in the late twelfth century, but the site of this church was probably much older.

The Northern Approach from Drumcondra and Glasnevin

the northern approach

Coming from the north, a visitor to the medieval city would have passed through an extensive suburb called Oxmantown, so called from the 'Ostmen' (Hiberno-Norse descendants of the Vikings) who went to live there after the Anglo-Norman takeover in 1170. The grid pattern of streets focused on present-day Church Street is an indication of planning to create house plots of a fairly uniform shape and size. Such planning was easier to achieve where the lie of the land was not too hilly. Here the dominant feature was St Mary's Abbey (now on the north side of the street appropriately called Mary's Abbey), a Cistercian monastery founded in the mid twelfth century. This was originally a Savigniac house associated with the Savigniac order, a Benedictine reform movement that began in Normandy. Its foundation in 1139 is one of many indications of French influence in Dublin before 1170. All of the Savigniac houses merged with the Cistercians in 1147–8, so that

View of Oxmantown from the south-east incorporating St Mary's Abbey, *c.* 1450, painted by Stephen Conlin. The Pill, being the estuary of the River Bradogue, together with an ocean-going ship, is visible in the left foreground.

42

Dublin acquired a monastery of that order in a very unusual suburban location with its own private harbour called The Pill (near present-day Ormond Square). The monks' chapter-house (meeting room) can still be seen today in Meetinghouse Lane. There was just one parish church on the north side of the Liffey, St Michan's, traditionally said to have been founded in 1095. Its unusual dedication may be a variant of Cainnech, patron of the early Christian monastery at Finglas. Serving all the people of the northside suburb, this church and its burial-ground were relatively large. The famous naturally mummified bodies in its crypt, however, date from a much later period.

Left: A section of the scale-model, looking south with Christ Church Cathedral in the foreground. The model shows clearly that even the main streets in the city centre were very narrow, with buildings set close together on plots of roughly equal size.

Right: Reconstruction of a late medieval street at Dublinia, featuring the Corpus Christi procession in the distance. The upper floor of some of the half-timbered houses is jettied outwards over the street to give extra living space.

On the opposite side of the main north-south street and fronting on to the River Liffey was St Saviour's Priory, a Dominican friary founded in 1224 (**17**). When approaching the only bridge across the Liffey from the north side a small chapel (**18**) would have come into view, a common facility for medieval travellers at major river-crossings. This particular example dates from soon after 1348, the year in which the Black Death first struck Ireland, an event that must have played a significant part in the spread of pious works in the late Middle Ages.

The land on the south side had been reclaimed from the river during the course of the thirteenth century. Again the street pattern is fairly regular. Gateways had been cut into the old north wall, one of which is the early thirteenth-century St Audoen's Arch (**19**). Beside Christ Church Cathedral on the crest of the ridge stood the parish church of St Michael the Archangel (now Dublinia itself) (**20**). This was originally a non-parochial church in the palace of the Hiberno-Norse bishops (Dublin became an *arch*bishopric in 1152). Thus the reconstructed city of *c.* 1500 depicted on the model had undergone many important changes before that date.

4

Learning from Later Maps

Maps and plans of the seventeenth and eighteenth

centuries record many medieval features and help modern

historians to reconstruct the past.

Maps were made in the Middle Ages, but they were not so common as they later became. Classical Latin *mappa* meant 'table cloth' or 'napkin' and by the thirteenth century *mappa mundi* ('map of the world') signified a circular depiction of the three 'known' continents of Africa, Asia and Europe, with Jerusalem at the centre. During the fourteenth and fifteenth centuries regular navigation and adventurous geographical exploration were aided by the portulan (navigational) charts used by sailors. The discovery of parts of the globe unfamiliar to Europeans continued apace in the sixteenth century and map-making became gradually more sophisticated. As a result, historians and historical geographers can learn much from post-medieval maps and plans, in order to compensate for the deficiencies or lack of medieval maps. It is thought likely that Dublin was first mapped during the reign of Queen Elizabeth I (1558–1603), but the earliest survivor dates from that of her successor.

Jacobean Dublin

King James VI of Scotland and I of England (1603–25) inaugurated the Stuart dynasty in his adopted country after the death of the childless Elizabeth. His name in Latin – still the language of intellectual pursuits – was Jacobus, from which we get the adjective 'Jacobean'.

A London tailor by profession, John Speed had taken up cartography and history in his spare time. His growing reputation as a map-maker had

Speed's map of Dublin. In the vicinity of Christ Church Cathedral, which is shown very small, it is possible to identify the church of St Michael the Archangel (now the site of Dublinia), the High Cross and the pillory.

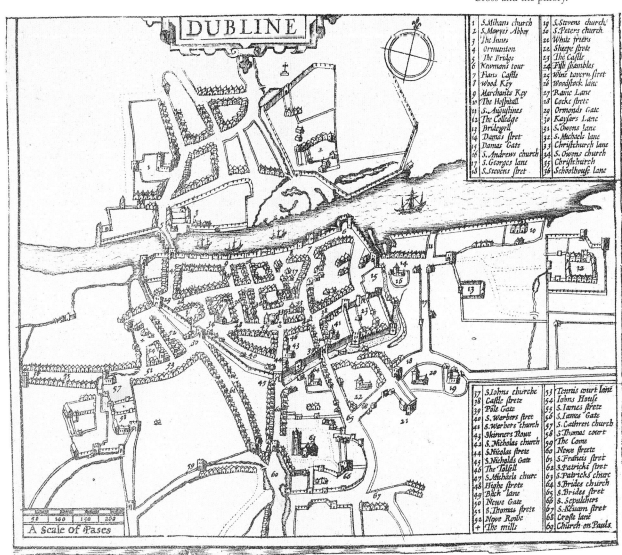

DUBLINE

1	S.Mihans church
2	S.Moryes Abbey
3	The Innes
4	Ormunton
5	The Bridge
6	Newmans tour
7	Fians Castle
8	Wood Key
9	Marchants Key
10	The Hospitall
11	S.Augustines
12	The Colledge
13	Bridewell
14	Damas stret
15	Damas Gate
16	S.Andrews church
17	S.Georges lane
18	S.Stevens stret
19	S.Stevens church
20	S.Peters church
21	White friers
22	Sheepe strete
23	The Castle
24	Fish shambles
25	Wine tavern stret
26	Woodstock lane
27	Ranie Lane
28	Cocke strete
29	Ormonds Gate
30	Kaysars Lane
31	S.Owens lane
32	S.Michaels lane
33	Christchurch lane
34	S.Owens church
35	Christchurch
36	Schoolhouse Lane
37	S.Johns churche
38	Castle strete
39	Pole Gate
40	S.Warbers stret
41	S.Warbers church
42	Skinners Rowe
43	S.Nicholas church
44	S.Nicolas strete
45	S.Nicholds Gate
46	The Tolsell
47	S.Michaels churc
48	Highe strete
49	Back lane
50	Newe Gate
51	S.Thomas strete
52	Newe Rowe
+	The mills
53	Tennis court lent
54	Johns House
55	S.Iames strete
56	S.Iames Gate
57	S.Cathret church
58	S.Thomas cort
59	The Come
60	Newe strete
61	S.Francis stret
62	S.Patricks stret
63	S.Patricks churc
64	S.Brides church
65	S.Brides stret
66	S.Sepulchers
67	S.Keuan stret
68	Crofse lane
69	Church on Pauls

A scale of Paces

50   100   150   200

earned the approval of the late queen and his book of maps of the constituent regions of the 'three kingdoms' (of England, Ireland and Scotland) was probably conceived in the latter part of Elizabeth's reign. The publication of *The Theatre of the Empire of Great Britaine* ..., with its imperialist connotations, coincided with the plantation of Ulster and with the expansionist policies of James's government.

Speed's bird's-eye view engraved (in Amsterdam) in 1610 shows a city that had hardly grown since the end of the Middle Ages, though many medieval features had already disappeared, partly or even completely, especially the monasteries and hospitals. Drawn to a scale of approximately 1:10,500, Speed's famous map was probably drafted a few years earlier either by the author himself or by an unknown person. The gaps in the building line near the Winetavern Street – Wood Quay corner may reflect damage caused by the great explosion of 1597, when casks of gunpowder that were being unloaded and carted up to the castle were accidentally ignited. The defensive wall along the quays has breaks to allow access to ships moored alongside.

Speed's map is inaccurate in many respects. For example, street widths tend to be exaggerated and the number of houses seriously under-represented. Like many European towns and cities, Dublin had probably still not recovered fully from the depopulation caused by outbreaks of plague in and since 1348. Another cause of decay had been the closure of all the monasteries by *c.* 1540 and the demolition of many of their buildings. Some monastic sites had been converted to other uses: St Saviour's Priory (Dominican) had become the Inns of Court (no. 3), All Saints' Priory (Augustinian) had become Trinity College (no. 12), and St Thomas's Abbey (Augustinian) had been secularised as Thomascourt (no. 58).

Restoration Dublin

In the year 1660, after the experimental Commonwealth period dominated by Oliver Cromwell, the Stuart monarchy was restored to power in the person of Charles II (1660–85). In Dublin this was the period when the city began to expand eastwards after many decades of virtual stagnation.

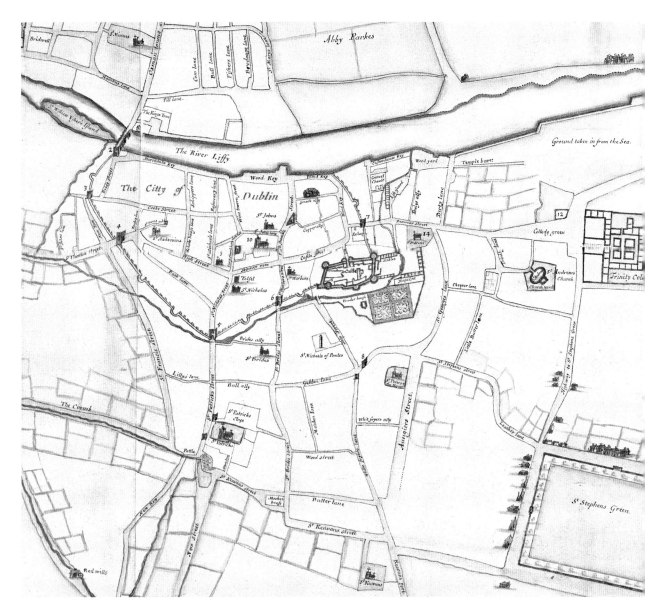

Sir Bernard de Gomme's map of the city and suburbs of Dublin in 1673 emphasises military considerations and shows the medieval walls, gates and castle basically intact. De Gomme was the royal engineer-in-chief who was sent to investigate the defensive needs of the city and to design a fort on its seaward side. The historical reason for the survey was the Third Anglo-Dutch War of 1672–4, before the threat from Louis XIV's France brought about an alliance between the two smaller countries.

De Gomme's map of the city and suburbs of Dublin (detail). This shows a much greater expanse of reclaimed ground on both sides of the River Liffey, including a street named Temple Barr, now in the city's cultural quarter.

47

Gabriel Beranger's view of the round tower of St Michael le Pole *c.* 1770, with a schoolhouse in the foreground. Recent archaeological excavations have shown that the tower had stood on a square base at the west end of the early church.

The familiar outline of the medieval defences is clearly visible, though not very accurately drawn. The old inner north wall is represented only by St Audoen's Arch, but the six principal gates were still standing. The castle, with its drawbridge and internal buildings, was to survive for another eleven years until the great fire of 1684. Some of the extramural gates are shown as well, including one due west of St Patrick's Cathedral.

In the very centre of the walled city was the Tholsel, opposite Christ Church Cathedral and likewise situated at the main crossroads marked by

Front Square, Trinity College showing the Dining Hall in the background and the Campanile (Bell Tower) in the foreground. Recent excavations nearby uncovered a number of burials thought to be those of the monks of All Saints' Priory.

the High Cross. This building was the city's administrative headquarters and its name, borrowed from English usage, denotes a toll-paying station. The early fourteenth-century Tholsel – probably a six-bay half-timbered structure whose size was underestimated by de Gomme – was demolished soon after 1673 and the site of its successor is now the Peace Garden opposite Christ Church Cathedral.

Other medieval remains that can be seen are the two cathedrals, most of the parish churches, and a

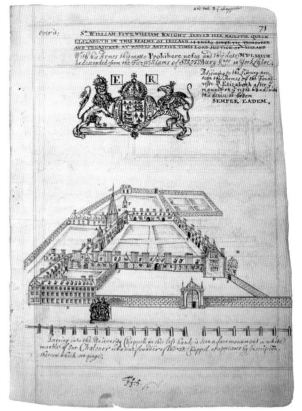

Early view of Trinity College from the west, showing the tower of All Saints' Priory incorporated in the north range of the main quadrangle. Financial records show that Trinity College opened its doors to students in January 1594.

number of natural and artificial watercourses. The most fascinating detail is the round tower of the church of St Michael le Pole. Shown here as a free-standing monument from a remote time in the past, this remnant from the Middle Ages was damaged by lightning and finally demolished in the late eighteenth century. Among the post-medieval features is Trinity College, occupying the site of the Augustinian priory of All Saints. By 1673 St Stephen's Green had been laid out for development purposes and the first houses had been built.

Georgian Dublin

The Hanoverian dynasty, originating in northern Germany, was installed in 1714 in an effort to guarantee a Protestant succession in the united kingdoms

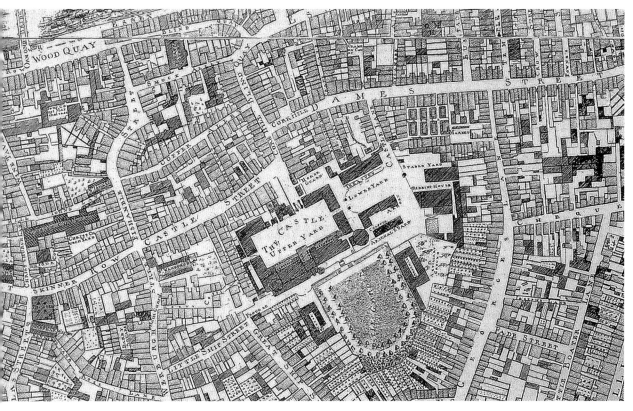

Extract from Rocque's map of Dublin. The garden situated behind Dublin Castle, on the site of the Black Pool, is shown here fully established in the shape of its modern successor.

Opposite page:
Illustrated map of medieval Dublin by Peter Walsh. The colour version pictured here was issued in 1988. A series of illustrations depicting aspects of medieval life, including a water conduit and a pillory (see overleaf), frame the map to left and right.

of England (and Wales), Ireland (since 1541) and Scotland (since 1603). As it happened, the first four kings, spanning the period 1714–1830, were all called George, giving rise to the architectural term 'Georgian'.

John Rocque's map published in 1756 shows the early Georgian city before the remodelling undertaken by the Wide Streets Commissioners. The commission was appointed by an act of parliament two years later to widen existing streets and to lay out new ones, starting with Parliament Street. The chief value of Rocque's map for medieval scholars lies in its depiction of the pattern of building plots in the oldest parts of the city.

Of English and French parentage, John Rocque was a professional map-maker and his stay in Ireland has been described as 'perhaps the only successful self-employed professional visit ever made to Ireland by a cartographer of European repute'. Rocque came to Dublin having already mapped Paris, London and Rome, and he produced the first detailed survey of Ireland's foremost city to a scale of 1:2,400. Four years later he published a map of County Dublin.

On Rocque's map of the city the medieval street pattern is still clearly visible. A good example is the curving alignment of streets in the Aungier Street area, representing the ecclesiastical enclosure associated with the much earlier Gaelic monastery of Dubhlinn. Yet the Anglo-Norman walls and gates barely feature at all, except as property boundaries such as that between Back Lane and Francis Street. All the surviving medieval parish churches had been partially or completely rebuilt by 1756, whereas the two cathedrals were not comprehensively restored until the following century.

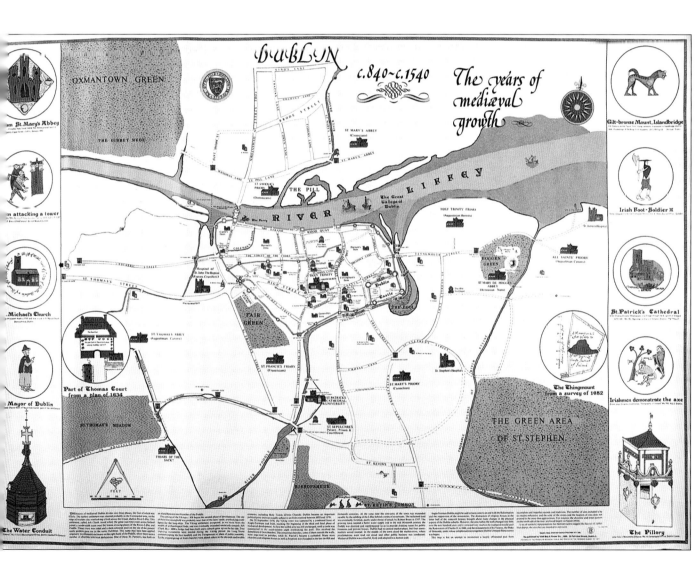

Past and Present

Detailed map of medieval Dublin. This map enables the user to understand the position of medieval features in relation to the modern cityscape. The 1939 base map (in grey) itself predates radical road widening and other developments of recent years.

The Friends of Medieval Dublin, founded as a study group in 1976, saw an immediate need for a comprehensive map of the medieval city. Two versions were produced, an illustrated one by Peter Walsh (1977) and a more detailed one by Howard Clarke (1978). Both maps were published by the Ordnance Survey of Ireland and Clarke's map has been reissued in a revised edition by the Royal Irish Academy.

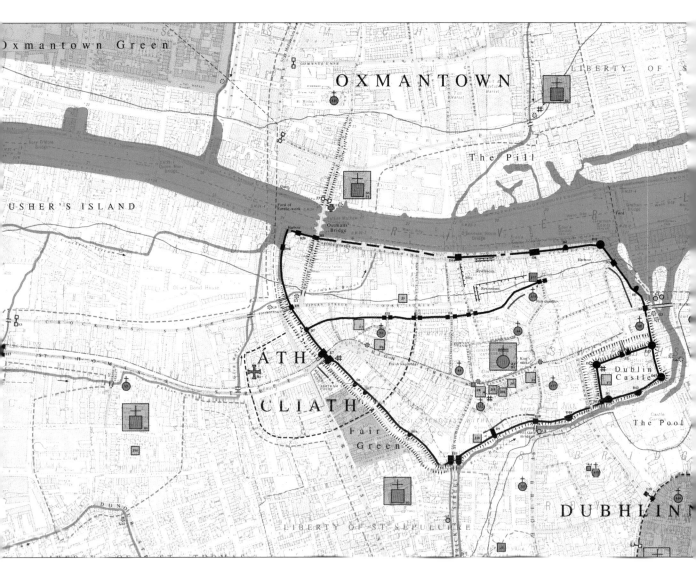

The first modern attempt to produce a map of medieval Dublin, by JS Sloane, was published in *The Irish Builder* in 1882. Before the days of scientific archaeology and when only a few collections of medieval documents had appeared in print, such a task presented many practical problems. Not surprisingly there were serious misconceptions, in particular about the course of the city walls.

Under the stimulus of archaeological investigations, beginning with the castle cross-block in 1961–2, more scientific approaches laid the groundwork for these two new maps. The illustrated one was designed to create an impression of how the city looked; the detailed one for research purposes. The latter was superimposed on a 1939 Ordnance Survey base map drawn to a scale of 1:2,500 (slightly smaller than Rocque's), which had the historical advantage of showing streets, lanes and property boundaries that no longer existed, or that had been changed out of all recognition, by the late 1970s.

5

Government

Medieval Dublin was an administrative
and judicial centre, both for the lordship of Ireland as a whole
and as a municipality governing itself in accordance with
a charter of urban liberties.

The central theme of this chapter is 'liberty', a word with many connotations in the Middle Ages. First of all the citizens of Dublin were endowed by kings of England with the liberty to administer many, though not all, aspects of public life in and around the city. Secondly, to this end, they were granted a territorial liberty inside which they held power and set up their own court. Thirdly, because this territory and these powers overlapped with those of some of the great churchmen, private territorial liberties were carved out of the city's own liberty in the early thirteenth century. Fourthly a comparatively rare liberty was granted to the citizens of Dublin in 1229 – that of electing a mayor (Latin *maior*) to represent their interests with regard to the outside world. Thereby Dublin, like London, attained the highest ranking among the urban communities of Britain and Ireland at that time. By the sixteenth century, proud Dubliners were conscious of their city's high status, most notably the author Richard Stanihurst who wrote in glowing terms of its natural and man-made attributes.

Municipal Self-government

Dublin was one of a number of royal towns in medieval Ireland, that is, its overlord was in principle the king of England. The essence of the 'freedom' that was valued so highly by medieval townspeople was self-government. In much of northern Europe the usual Latin word for a townsman was *burgensis*, 'burgess', since he inhabited a *burgus*, 'town'. In practice this term came to refer to the more privileged members of the urban community who enjoyed full rights of citizenship. The administrative competence of royal officials was progressively reduced over time and the privileges enjoyed by the burgesses came to be embodied in charters of urban liberties. These documents in turn stimulated the citizens to produce and to preserve their own archives.

The city received its charters directly from successive kings, in contrast to the many small towns whose overlords were lay and ecclesiastical aristocrats. Dublin's first royal charter as an independent town was granted by Henry II's son, John, in his capacity as lord of Ireland. It dates from 1192 and is still preserved in the archives of Dublin City Council.

The late twelfth-century charter contains a standard list of urban liberties, going back via Bristol's to those of London. A formal link between Dublin and Bristol was established by Henry II in the course of his visit to Ireland in 1171–2. In order to convert Dublin into the main focus of loyalty to the English crown in Ireland, the king entrusted the process of colonisation to the

Opposite page: Civic Window at Dublinia, designed by George Walsh in 1993. The left panel shows the civic sword, the provost's seal (used before the election of the first mayor in 1229), signs of the zodiac, knights on campaign and part of the city's skyline.

Far left: The great seal of King Henry II. In an age of widespread illiteracy, even among the powerful and wealthy, medieval people did not sign documents. Instead, they attached their personal seal, so as to authenticate the contents.

Left: John as king of England playing with his dogs. King John is generally reputed to have been a 'bad' king, best remembered for accepting the terms of the Magna Carta in 1215 out of political weakness. Here we see his more amiable side.

Right: The 1192 charter of liberties. The charter is written in Latin, in a typical formal hand of the late twelfth century. The ties at the base once held the wax seal, which does not survive.

Below: The charter of King Henry II, dating from the winter of 1171–2, granting the city of Dublin to the men of Bristol, who were to enjoy their traditional liberties here.

burgesses of Bristol, a town where he had spent several months as a boy during the civil war of his predecessor's reign. This grant of Dublin to the men of Bristol had been recorded in an earlier charter, the oldest document now preserved in Dublin City Archives.

One of the citizens' most important liberties was to have their own court, known as the hundred (an ancient subdivision of some English counties), which met once a week. Matters relating to landownership and to debt were dealt with there. All 'foreign' (non-Dublin) merchants were put at a disadvantage as traders, thus ensuring a local monopoly. For example, no foreign merchant was allowed to run a wine tavern except on board a ship in the harbour. Citizens of Dublin were free to contract marriages for themselves, their sons, daughters and widows without having to get permission from a lord.

The 1192 charter of liberties is a very formal document drawn up in the normal language of recording, Latin, much of it written as one long sentence. In order to convey a sense of its true nature, two clauses and part of a third will now be given, together with a translation:

§ 15 *et quod nullus extraneus mercator emat infra civitatem de homine extraneo blada vel coria vel lanam nisi de civibus et quod nullus extraneus habeat tabernam de vino nisi in navi …*; 'and that no foreign merchant shall buy within the city from a foreigner corn or hides or wool except from citizens, and that no foreigner shall have a wine tavern except on a ship …'.

§ 16 *et quod nullus extraneus vendat pannos in civitate ad decisionem*; 'and that no foreigner shall sell cloth in the city by retail'.

§ 17 *et quod nullus extraneus mercator moretur in villa cum mercibus suis pro mercibus suis vendendis nisi per xl dies*; 'and that no foreign merchant shall stay in the town with his wares, in order to sell his wares, for more than forty days'.

Wine jug from the Saintonge area of south-west France, probably brought to Dublin via Bordeaux in the thirteenth century. Found at Winetavern Street, the body of the jug is decorated using a combed technique and the green glaze is typical for the period.

The Liberties of Dublin

Probably soon after 1170 the city's 'liberty' or area of jurisdiction was marked out on the ground. These boundaries north and south of the River Liffey are described at the beginning of the 1192 charter. In all, nearly 15.5 square kilometres (6 square miles) of territory were granted by order of King Henry II. The city was in principle self-governing within these boundaries, though the king always retained certain financial and legal rights as its superior lord.

The liberties and free customs, such as exemption from trial by combat (a method of settling disputes suited to knights and other trained fighting

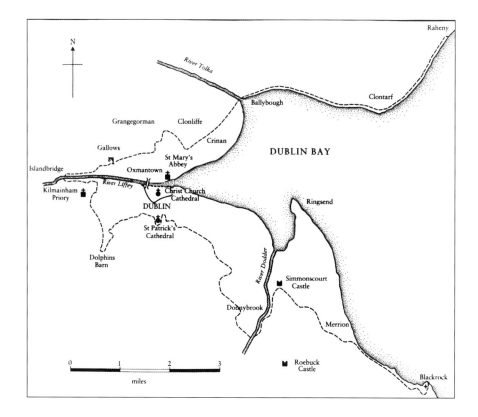

Right: Map of the boundaries of the liberty of Dublin. The boundaries included the inner part of Dublin Bay and inland as far as the high tide mark at Islandbridge. The irregular boundary line reflects that of property ownership at that time.

Below: Franchise roll of free citizens. 'Free' citizens were those who enjoyed full rights to citizenship. As in other towns and cities, large numbers of the inhabitants, including most women, were not free in this political sense.

men) and the right to prove contracts by their own oaths, were to be enjoyed by all fully enfranchised citizens of Dublin. As plaintiffs and as defendants they attended the hundred court of the city, which was presided over originally by the royal provost (a term that means 'someone placed before or above others') and, from 1229, by the mayor. Most punishments took the form of fines, but two dungeons in the basement of the south tower of Newgate came to serve as the city's prison. In 1526 this jail held seven prisoners: four for indebtedness, two for felony and one for trespass.

One complication arose from the fact that great churchmen held land inside the city's liberty. In this period misdemeanours committed by priests, monks and nuns were dealt with in ecclesiastical courts. During the thirteenth century five private, ecclesiastical liberties were carved out of the city's greater

58

Left: Sexual misconduct was not unknown even on the part of those living in enclosed religious houses. Medieval priests ministering in parishes were commonly living openly as married men or had clandestine relations with women.

liberty: those of Christ Church Cathedral, St Patrick's Cathedral, St Sepulchre's Palace, St Thomas's Abbey and St Mary's Abbey. Three great lords – the archbishop of Dublin, the abbot of St Thomas's and the abbot of St Mary's – acquired the right to try laymen as well, to levy fines and, if necessary, to hang criminals on their own gallows. We happen to know, for example, that the abbot of St Thomas's was holding his court every fortnight in the early fourteenth century, suggesting that there was a regular supply of judicial business. The medieval archbishops had a gallows about half way along The Coombe, on the western boundary of the liberty of St Sepulchre; in those days, hanging people was a public spectacle! Since most of these private liberties were located in the general area of St Patrick's Cathedral, that part of the city is still known today as The Liberties.

Below: This portrait of Archbishop Henry Blund 'de Londres' comes from the Waterford charter roll. It was painted about a century after his death in 1228 and cannot be taken as an accurate likeness of his physical features.

The northside liberty of St Mary's Abbey occupied a large area either side of present-day Mary Street. Indeed, from time to time its status was a subject of dispute, as in 1488 when the mayor was conducting a party of important citizens on horseback along the boundary of the city's own liberty, in a ritual known as 'riding the franchises'.

Twice on this occasion they were accosted by the abbot and his monks, but the mayor, Thomas Meyler, stood his ground. In the English dialect of the day he announced: 'Nay, for by our boke [charter] when we did retorne bakward fromm the Tolkan' [River Tolka] we shold haue rid to Our Lady Churche of Ostmanneby [St Mary's Abbey in Oxmantown]'.

Local Laws and Customs

Whereas a charter of urban liberties would be drawn up in terms of broad principles, the citizens themselves came to formulate their own laws and customs. Those of Dublin are known to us from an early fourteenth-century Norman-French copy in the Chain Book, so called because it was secured by a chain in the Tholsel (effectively the city court and council chamber) for public consultation. One special local custom was the official measurement of time and by 1466 there was a public clock on top of the Tholsel, probably the first of its kind in Ireland. Mechanical clocks in the Middle Ages normally had only an hour hand and may not have been very accurate. Until comparatively recently, time was measured locally without reference to any national or international standard. Thus fifteenth-century Dubliners would have kept their own time in practice.

The first folio of the text of the laws and customs of Dublin is preserved in the Chain Book. French was the international language of western Europe during the high Middle Ages.

These local laws and customs were drawn up initially in the first half of the thirteenth century, at a time when Norman-French was commonly spoken in Dublin. For professional reasons merchants needed to be literate, though not necessarily in Latin. At its weekly meetings the hundred court would have dealt with infringements of these laws and the fines that were levied would have provided a useful source of income to the municipality. Some punishments were more dramatic: causing a whole street to

Waterford *c.* 1370, the earliest illustration of an Irish town. The trading ships are single-masted and have fighting platforms ('castles') fore and aft. Rabbits are believed to have been introduced into Ireland by the Anglo-Normans.

burn down, for example, might result in arrest and then being thrown into the middle of the fire!

Three trades in particular were regulated by local laws – those of the bakers, the butchers and the fishmongers. Bread was so much the staff of life that loaves were stamped with the bakers' own names, while meat and fish traders had to be controlled for reasons of public hygiene. Brewing was important, too, and women brewers (brewing ale was a traditionally female occupation as a kind of cottage industry that did not require great physical strength) normally paid 2s. a year for their licence and were fined 15d. for making inferior ale. Traditional ale was made without the beneficial properties of hops and would not have conformed with modern tastes. The addition of hops was a late medieval innovation that spread only slowly across northern parts of Europe. The far graver offences of insulting the mayor outside the Tholsel incurred a fine of 40s. and of actually hitting him £40. Not to be outdone, Waterford's local laws and customs – the only other complete set to have survived – were modelled closely on those of Dublin.

Crime and Punishment

In many parts of Europe by the late twelfth century there were four main types of jurisdiction – royal, ecclesiastical, seigneurial and municipal. A chartered town or city of the kind that Dublin became in 1192 had control over most legal matters involving lay men and women through its municipal court (the hundred), but serious crimes such as arson and rape were dealt with in the king's court. Dublin's area of jurisdiction included parts of the surrounding countryside, where corn stealing or even highway robbery might occur.

Trial and execution for a serious crime. The top panel shows a bound prisoner being tried before a judge as a clerk records the proceedings. The lower panel shows two prisoners being taken to their place of execution.

Unfortunately no proceedings of the hundred court have survived from this period and most of the details about individual legal cases concerning medieval Dubliners are preserved in the records of royal courts. Here are two examples, both of them homicide cases taken from the year 1311. First, on a ship moored in the harbour a man called Richard del Shoppe was attacked with a big stick by Adam de Cokerford. Richard used the ship's mast as a shield

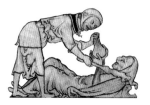

Left to right: Two 'citizens' being punished in the pillory at Dublinia. This form of punishment was taken rather more seriously in the Middle Ages, to the extent that it was reported in the late sixteenth century that missiles directed at the offenders were polluting the public water supply.

Drawing of a man stealing corn. Standing crops in open fields, fruit trees in orchards and, in Mediterranean countries, grapes on the vine were particularly vulnerable towards harvest time and measures against theft were commonly taken.

Highway robbery in the thirteenth century: a man being struck down with a cudgel and robbed. In the Middle Ages, with no police force, crimes of violence were commonplace.

and then struck Adam with his cutlass, killing him. Nevertheless Richard was pardoned because the jurors said that he was acting in self-defence. Secondly some sailors, among them Englishmen, killed a man named Robert Thurstayn. Five were found guilty and hanged. Afterwards two of these men, having been taken down from the gallows presumed dead, were removed by cart to Kilmainham for burial. They were still alive, however, and sought refuge in the local church; they, too, were subsequently pardoned.

Fully enfranchised citizens would normally have been fined by the hundred court if found guilty of breaking the law, though inability to pay a fine or to repay a debt might result in a spell in the city prison. Prisoners of this type were not usually locked up for long periods, unlike political prisoners with aristocratic backgrounds who were sometimes confined for years in Dublin Castle. In the thirteenth century a jail stood near the city wall between Werburgh Street and the castle (on a site now occupied by an employment exchange), but in the late Middle Ages the south tower of Newgate was adapted as a suitably secure place for this purpose. Jailers were appointed by the city authorities and were paid in relation to the number of prisoners (usually small) held in custody. Prisoners were chained by the legs and by the neck, smaller equipment being used for children. The use of part of Newgate as a jail (as in London) illustrates the way in which town gates often

Left: Seventeenth-century stocks from Christ Church Cathedral, preserved in the crypt. Less severe than the pillory, the stocks restrained the offender by the legs and he or she remained seated. Each jurisdiction would have had its own pillory and stocks.

had uses additional to the obvious military ones: as toll stations, as residences, as storage places, as meeting-rooms, and for enforcing the curfew at night-time.

Minor offences, including moral lapses such as committing adultery and fornicating in public, were punished by exposure to abuse and ridicule in the pillory, which stood at the crossroads south-east of Christ Church Cathedral (outside the present day Lord Edward public house). Here the offender's head and hands were locked in a wooden frame, known as a pillory, which allowed vengeful people to pelt him or her with eggs, rotten vegetation and the like. Even today we talk figuratively about a person being 'pilloried'. Other forms of punishment were to be locked up in a confined space about the size of a large dog kennel and to be horse-drawn through the streets on a hurdle (a wicker screen). This was designed to humiliate rather than to harm; road surfaces were bumpy and generous measures of dirt and noise would have ensured a suitable level of misery for the offender.

Punishment in the lock-up and on the hurdle. In the upper panel two men, one resisting, are about to be locked up. In the lower panel the driver urges his horse, while the weighing scales indicate that justice has been done.

Rulers of Dublin

In the early days of the English colony in Ireland, Dublin was governed by royal officials headed by a provost. Then in 1229 the burgesses and freemen were granted the right to elect a mayor each year and two provosts, later called bailiffs, assisted him. The city council consisted of twenty-four prominent citizens, mostly merchants. These men were unpaid, but there were also professional officers such as the clerk, the recorder and the treasurer who probably lived off a combination of fees and salaries.

The first mayor of Dublin was Richard Muton and the names of all his successors (called lord mayors from 1665) are known. The mayor represented the citizens in relation to other authorities, presided over the city council and city court, and executed the decisions made by the councillors. A political crisis such as the threatened Scottish attack in 1317 would call for special powers of leadership. The provosts or bailiffs assisted him in many ways – collecting the city rent due to the crown, acting as coroners, enrolling contracts, supervising the seizure of confiscated goods and stray animals, and intervening in disputes between masters and apprentices.

These stylised portraits of the mayors of Dublin, Waterford, Cork and Limerick, from the Waterford charter roll, are merely symbolic. Other important towns were Galway, Kilkenny and New Ross, none of which had a mayor in the Middle Ages.

One of the most colourful mayors of Dublin in the Middle Ages was Geoffrey Morton (1303–4). Like so many other mayors he was a merchant, trading in Scotland, Flanders and Gascony (the wine-producing region in south-western France that was linked politically with England). During his mayoral year he fell foul of royal officials and spent thirty-six days in prison altogether, before being removed from office. Some years later he got permission to collect special murage tolls for repairing the city walls, but abused his authority by extorting money unfairly. He also engaged in illegal building operations near Bridge Gate.

The mayoral year usually ran from Michaelmas to Michaelmas (29 September, the feast of St Michael the Archangel), thus coinciding with the fiscal year operated by the exchequer. Like those of other major Irish towns, the mayor of Dublin had in principle to take an oath of fealty (loyalty) to the king of England. Since the king was hardly ever in Ireland, the justiciar or lieutenant received the oath on the king's behalf. Engravings featuring Sir Henry Sidney, one of Elizabeth I's deputies in Ireland, were published in 1581 and represent the earliest views of the city.

Above: The king receiving the homage of the mayor and bailiffs of Waterford. In practice, the oath of loyalty was normally taken to the justiciar, the king's representative in Ireland. The municipal institutions of Waterford were closely modelled on those of Dublin.

Right: The departure of Sir Henry Sidney, Queen Elizabeth's 'deputy' in Ireland in the 1560s and 1570s, from Dublin Castle. The castle's architecture is somewhat fanciful, but Sidney is known to have restored and modernised it as an administrative centre.

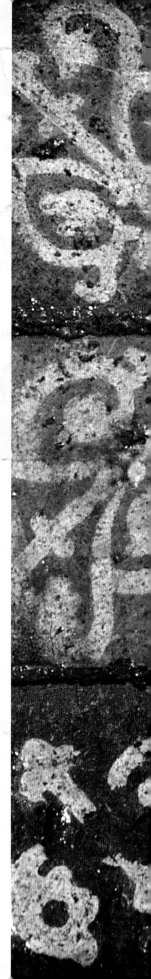

6

Guilds and Crafts

Merchants and craftworkers
organised themselves into religious and social associations
called guilds, which satisfied a number
of distinct needs.

Although we sometimes talk about the 'urban community' as an entity in itself, in practice medieval townspeople tended to form themselves into associations in order to defend and to promote perceived common interests. These interests were normally economic and social, but they could have political and religious dimensions as well. Since merchants, especially long-distance ones dealing in exotic goods, had greater opportunities to acquire wealth and thereby political status, they were among the first to form such associations or guilds (gilds). The word 'guild' contains the idea of payment (compare German *Geld*, 'money') and may relate to an early feature of these associations – communal drinking and feasting – for which each member paid a contribution. In the course of time craftworkers formed similar associations, but their political status in most towns and cities was lower than that of the merchants. In large continental cities fierce power struggles occurred between, and even within, trade and craft guilds, but there is little direct evidence of these in the case of Dublin.

The Guild Merchant

Previous page: Medieval tiles from Christ Church Cathedral. During the restoration programme of 1871–8, hundreds of decorated tiles were discovered. They were subsequently relaid at the eastern end of the south aisle in the Chapel of St Laud, where they form sixty-three separate patterns.

Left: Marginal sketch of Nevin of Connacht on the Guild Merchant roll. The standard membership subscription of 9s. is shown by a series of vertical strokes by each name. Nevin's portrait occurs at 1232–3, soon after the initial Anglo-Norman conquest of Connacht.

Right: Marginal sketch of Robert Godson of Gloucester on the Guild Merchant roll. His name occurs at 1229–30, the year in which the citizens of Dublin were granted permission by King Henry III to elect a mayor as the chief officer of the city council.

The oldest guild in medieval Dublin (and in Ireland) was the Guild Merchant. To start with it was a general guild with a wide membership of both residents and outsiders. In the late Middle Ages, however, this guild came to represent those who were professional merchants and its members were clearly linked to the city council.

By his charter of 1171–2 Henry II wanted to encourage the settlement of English merchants in Dublin, under the supervision of the men of Bristol, by granting them trading privileges. As a result many hundreds of merchants and craftsmen flocked to Dublin. Particularly large numbers came from the

west midlands and south-centre of England, and the extreme south of Wales. Among the most prominent towns and cities as places of origin are Bristol, Cardiff, Gloucester, London, Winchester and Worcester. From *c.* 1190 to 1265 their names, and very occasionally their portraits or symbols, are recorded on the Guild Merchant roll. Altogether about 8,400 names occur, but not all these people were resident in Dublin; many were outsiders trading there. This is a membership list that is still preserved in the city archives as the earliest document of its type from anywhere in Britain or Ireland. New members, only three of whom were women, paid an entry fee that was eventually standardised at 9s., or nine times the ground rent for a burgage plot.

As in many other big towns and cities, the municipal council grew out of the Guild Merchant, in Dublin in the early thirteenth century. The original headquarters of both the guild and the council was the Guild Hall in Winetavern Street, overlooking the river and the new land that was being

Left: Merchants waiting on a quayside for the arrival of ships. Trading voyages in the Middle Ages often took weeks or even months and a merchant who had invested in a particular ship would naturally be anxious to see it arrive back in port. Note the merchants' worried faces and wringing of hands.

reclaimed from it. By an accident of history, the Guild Hall occupied part of the much larger site of today's Civic Offices. This building was replaced in the fourteenth century by another called the Tholsel, which stood on the corner of Nicholas Street and Skinners' Row (now Christchurch Place). Here in an upper room the late medieval Guild Merchant held its assemblies four times a year, paying the city authorities an annual rent of 3s. 8d. for the privilege.

Craft Guilds

Craft guilds were exclusive organisations representing specialised groups such as dyers, smiths dealing in iron goods, and weavers. In their activities there was a strong element of the protectionism that is a characteristic of local monopolies. Evidence for the craft guilds survives from the fifteenth century onwards, a time of economic decline or stagnation, but their origins probably go back further in some cases. By the end of the fifteenth century

Above: Effigy of a woman in Christ Church Cathedral, early thirteenth century, probably from the west of England. She wears a 'pill-box' head-dress, a barbette beneath her chin and a long plain tunic breaking slightly over her feet, where a dog lies among foliage.

Right: Blacksmiths at their work. To the left a furnace is kept stoked with fuel and its temperature is regulated by a pair of bellows. To the right two smiths beat alternately on a lump of iron held in position on an anvil.

Below: Floor tiles of local manufacture from the thirteenth century. The lion's head and foliate designs would have formed part of a larger pattern. *In situ* tile pavements are rare in Ireland and are found only in a religious context.

there were almost thirty craft and trade guilds in the city. These guilds had an assembly hall and often provided financial support for one or more priests to sing masses in a private chapel in one of the parish churches.

Above all, the craft guilds established and maintained standards of workmanship, by requiring each new recruit to execute a 'masterpiece' that needed to have the wardens' approval. They were usually governed by one or two masters, assisted by two wardens. These officials had the right to inquire into all offences committed by guild members in the city, to examine apprentices after the customary seven years, to arrest runaway apprentices, and to regulate prices and wages. Apprentices often made up part of their master's household, being accommodated in garrets and other confined spaces. An unknown proportion would have been the sons of qualified masters.

At the same time craft guilds fulfilled longstanding charitable and social functions. They gave practical assistance to members in times of personal difficulty (for example, when someone's house burnt down),

Women carding, spinning and weaving. Women performed a number of industrial jobs as a rule, especially in the production of cloth. Carding was the process whereby the wool fibres were combed out between two boards equipped with iron 'teeth' prior to spinning.

provided funeral expenses and support for widows, and funded elementary schools. Guilds held processions on the feast day of their patron saint and in Dublin, as in some other towns, the various crafts were responsible for portraying particular biblical characters in the Corpus Christi Day pageant. Some guilds admitted women to more or less full membership in accordance with local custom, especially the widows of deceased members, and some accumulated property through bequests.

Above left: Jesus of Nazareth portrayed as an apprentice dyer. Lengths of cloth are being dyed in heated vats. That the historical Jesus was the son of a carpenter would have been well known, but here he is being linked with another common craft.

Above right: Boys playing at being at school, with the 'master' beating a pupil. There was a municipal schoolhouse in the narrow laneway off High Street still called Schoolhouse Lane. Elementary education was seen as being more appropriate for boys than for girls.

The Stonemason

Stonework or masonry was relatively expensive in the Middle Ages because of the cost of quarrying, transporting and cutting such heavy and resistant material. Dublin's local stone was calp, a dark-grey limestone that was difficult to use in a refined way. The nature of this stone is best seen in remaining portions of the city wall, including St Audoen's Arch in Cook Street, and in the crypt of Christ Church Cathedral. For this reason a certain amount of stone was imported from England and France for the doorways and windows of major buildings: for instance, Dundry stone from south of Bristol and Caen stone from central Normandy. Stonemasons enjoyed a higher status than most other craftsmen because of their skills and the scale of their building projects.

The durability of stone, as compared with that of timber, means that today we have an unbalanced view above ground of the built environment of the medieval city. Very large stone structures such as castles and cathedrals

Left: Doorway to the south transept of Christ Church Cathedral. Originally the north doorway, it was repositioned in the early nineteenth century. The round-headed arch and chevron decoration are typical features of late Romanesque architecture.

Bottom left: Keystone with human head made of imported English Dundry stone. Quarried near Bristol, Dundry stone was valued for its rich texture and durability. A large collection of loose stones survives in Christ Church Cathedral from the time of its restoration in the 1870s.

Below right: Stonemasons building the Tower of Babel. The attempted construction of this tower is described in Genesis and is associated with a confusion of languages. Medieval building sites would have been similarly confused and noisy, and some projects were clearly over-ambitious.

normally took many years to build: St Patrick's Cathedral, for example, needed about a quarter of a century to complete. Their biblical equivalent was the Tower of Babel. Medieval scaffolding was made from heavy timbers, with the result that a building site would have been doubly impressive. Winches were used to raise stone and other materials to the required level. Large numbers of semi-skilled and unskilled labourers would have worked on major projects.

Highly skilled stonemasons often moved from place to place with their tools. Professional masons were responsible for drawing moulding profiles, designing doorways and windows, determining the thickness of walls and other technical matters. The marks of individual masons, usually in abstract form, are sometimes found on medieval stonework; their purpose is uncertain but they enable architectural historians to trace the movements of some of these craftworkers. Occasionally their names are known as well: for example, we learn from a charter that a Master Walter was permanently employed as a mason of St Mary's Abbey in the middle of the thirteenth century.

The Leather-worker

Leather-working in the Middle Ages was divided into a number of different crafts: the cordwainer made shoes, the cobbler repaired them, the saddler made and repaired saddles, and the glover made gloves. A leather-worker would buy his hides from a tanner who tanned them with oak bark or oak galls (growths found on the trees), or from a whittawer who tawed skins into whitleather (white leather) using a dressing of alum and salt. Alum is a whitish, transparent mineral salt, which was difficult to obtain and therefore expensive. The papal states in central Italy were a major supplier in the Middle Ages.

Boy looking at life-sized reconstruction showing a shoemaker at Dublinia. Otherwise known as a cordwainer, the figure is working outside his shop using his knife as a tool. In the Middle Ages, knives would also have been used for food preparation and general household purposes.

74

Traditionally goods such as shoes were made to order at the craftsman's shop or shop window, but from the fourteenth century there is evidence of mass production for the market. In general medieval shops were similarly specialised places where people went for particular items. Sometimes small shops were grouped together and were called 'selds'.

The tanning of leather could be an unpleasant process since animal dung, fats or urine were often added to the mixture in which the hides were soaked. The precise formula would affect the colour of the final product. A constant supply of fresh water was also needed and medieval tanneries were preferably located outside the walls of a town or city. The more refined process of tawing made the hide softer as well as colourless.

Medieval footwear was made by the turnshoe technique, that is, the upper and the sole were stitched together inside out and then turned the right way round. A thin strip of leather called a rand was stitched between the upper and the sole along the lasting seam, thereby strengthening it and ensuring that the shoe was watertight. Pattens or overshoes made of leather or wood and attached to the shoe by straps gave added protection from the muddy lanes and streets. A pair of shoes might be repaired several times and a 'new' pair of children's shoes was sometimes made from worn-out adult ones recut to fit smaller feet. Shoes, ankle boots and full-sized boots were worn and were fastened either at the front or at the side.

High-quality gloves would have been made of softer leather and were worn, as might be expected, by men and women of high social standing. A pair of white gloves sometimes served instead of money as a relatively nominal annual rent for property. Peppercorns imported from farthest Asia were used for the same purpose in the Middle Ages, hence the term 'peppercorn rent'. Farm workers would have worn gloves made from more robust leather: for example, when handling tools or sheaves of corn.

Medieval saddles do not survive, but they were probably basically similar to modern ones. A light wooden frame would have formed the base, over which pieces of leather were stretched. The upward projecting part of the saddle at the front was called a pommel (from a word meaning 'little

From around 1300 a new, highly extravagant style of shoe called the poulaine (meaning 'Polish', Poland being the country of origin) became popular among fashion-conscious members of society. The toe was made very long and narrow, with the result that it had to be stuffed with moss and straw. Often the toe was so long that it was connected to a band at the knee by a small chain, to enable the wearer to walk!

apple') and assisted the rider when mounting or dismounting. William the Conqueror, the first Norman king of England, may have had an especially elaborate pommel on his saddle, for in 1087 he was fatally injured when thrown against it in the course of sacking the town of Mantes, near Paris. By that stage in his life, he was also extremely corpulent!

Below: Twelfth-century fragment of a wooden door or lid of a chest found at High Street. The hooked iron attachment may have functioned as a hinge or as a type of fastening.

Right: Iron spur found at Wood Quay. The earliest medieval spurs were of the prick type with a single spike at the back. The rowel spur was more sophisticated and effective, having a turning wheel of smaller spikes. Rowel spurs became more common in the thirteenth century.

FINDS BOX

Wood and Iron-working

Coopers, turners and smiths were craftsmen typical of medieval towns. Coopers were skilled in the manufacture of containers such as barrels, buckets and tubs. These were constructed using individual staves bound together with wooden or metal hoops fitted around the circumference; the base and lids of the vessels were simple discs of wood. This type of vessel rarely survives intact, but staves, hoops and bases are common finds from Dublin sites. Barrels of all shapes and sizes were used to contain, and to transport, anything from wine to butter.

Another specialist woodcraft was lathe turning, using a simple machine known as a pole lathe. Two types of evidence survive to illustrate the turning process. Firstly, there are the finished objects, which include wooden bowls, tool handles and lids, and secondly, manufacturing evidence, in the form of waste cores or tools. Iron-working was carried out by the smith, an important figure in medieval society. Aside from staples, chains and similar fittings made of wrought iron, the smith would be commissioned to make weapons and equestrian equipment, including horseshoes, spurs, bridle bits, cheek-pieces and harness mounts.

7

Trade

During our period Dublin continued to function
as a major trading centre, both with the surrounding countryside
and with other parts of western Europe.

Broadly speaking, the trade of the Viking Age (ninth to eleventh centuries) had extended over vast distances but had amounted to comparatively little in terms of bulk. The twelfth and thirteenth centuries, on the other hand, witnessed an enormous increase in the volume of trade in many parts of Europe, including Ireland. In particular considerable quantities of cloth (dyed and undyed), grain, pottery, timber, wine and wool were shipped from places of source to places of processing and consumption. By preference ships and boats were used for transporting bulky goods, being more cost-effective than carts and pack-animals. Ports such as Dublin were well positioned to participate in and to profit from all this trading activity, both local and long-distance. With the depopulation caused by plague epidemics in and after 1348, demand was obviously reduced, yet trade continued in a wide range of goods, partly because standards of living may have risen for the surviving population. Dublin's main problem seems to have been the physical difficulty of accessing the quays from the open sea owing to treacherous currents and sandbanks in the bay and river channel.

Ships in front of an English town. In Dublin, large ocean-going ships would have found it difficult to access the quays directly and goods were often unloaded on to smaller vessels at Dalkey harbour for transportation to the city.

The Local Market

All towns acted as local market centres, partly out of the necessity to bring in food from the surrounding countryside. A city such as Dublin would tend to dominate its economic hinterland and the area of the historic county contained no other fully-fledged towns. To the west and north (in the modern counties of Kildare and Meath) there was a fringe of small towns in the Middle Ages: Naas, Kildare, Athboy, Trim, Navan, Kells and Duleek.

There were, however, a number of market settlements in the neighbour-hood of Dublin: for example, Clondalkin, Rathcoole and Swords. At least for a period of time there were burgesses (holders of land by burgage tenure,

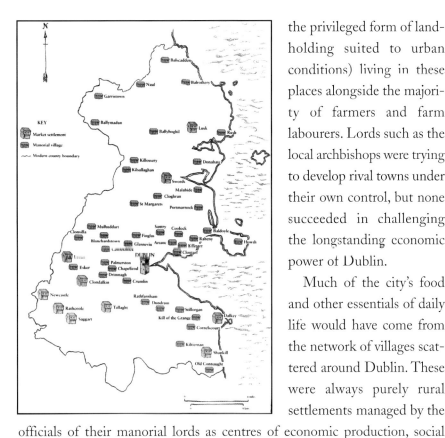

the privileged form of land-holding suited to urban conditions) living in these places alongside the majority of farmers and farm labourers. Lords such as the local archbishops were trying to develop rival towns under their own control, but none succeeded in challenging the longstanding economic power of Dublin.

Much of the city's food and other essentials of daily life would have come from the network of villages scattered around Dublin. These were always purely rural settlements managed by the officials of their manorial lords as centres of economic production, social organisation and judicial control. Grain, dairy products and freshwater fish were in constant demand. Irish tenants lived on many of these manors alongside the colonists.

Above: Sowing grain from a seed basket. After each harvest, enough grain had to be kept back for sowing either in the autumn or in the spring. It was stored in the granary, ideally stone-built to protect the grain from damp conditions and vermin.

Above left: Map of County Dublin showing manorial villages, some with market functions, in Dublin's hinterland. Many of the modern city's suburbs are based on former villages. Even today there are clues to their location, in particular a Protestant parish church.

Below: Women reaping and a man gathering sheaves. Reaping grain by hand with a sickle was back-breaking work often performed by women. The stubble left standing was used for thatching and as bedding for animals, or it was ploughed back into the soil.

Milking a cow. The milking of cows, together with other aspects of dairying such as butter making, were seen as women's work in many traditional cultures.

The International Market

By 1170 Dublin had been a centre of international trade for three centuries and it continued to function as one of Ireland's leading ports. After 1170 the direction of the city's trade shifted more firmly towards England, France, the Low Countries and northern Spain and slaves ceased to be an item of exchange. Every year foreign traders, some from as far away as Italy, would come to do business at the summer fair on Fair Green, which was situated just outside the great western defensive ditch, on the eastern side of present-day Francis Street, where the Iveagh Markets' building now stands.

As today, medieval international trade involved both exports and imports, but it is impossible to know how the balance of that

Shearing sheep in the countryside. The shearing of sheep was a physically demanding task usually performed by men. Irish wool was relatively coarse, but still a valuable national resource used as a cheaper alternative to finer English varieties.

trading activity fluctuated. By the late thirteenth century Dublin had become one of a small number of staple ports through which Irish wool, woolfells (fleeces) and hides passed and at which customs duty was charged for the benefit of the English crown. Other likely exports from Dublin were grain from the city's immediate hinterland; the furs of animals such as the hare, marten and squirrel; fish, especially hake, herring and salmon; and rough frieze cloth and linen.

Throughout northern Europe wine was a regular import and a tax on imported wine is mentioned in the 1192 charter of liberties. Wine was needed for the liturgy of the Church as well as for domestic consumption and the main street leading up from the quays was a drinking man's paradise – Winetavern Street. Most of Dublin's wine came probably from Gascony, whose chief port was Bordeaux. Salt was imported both from England and from western France, while fine cloth came from England and Flanders and iron ore from northern Spain. More exotic, light-weight products such as dyes, medicines and spices reached Dublin via long-distance trade routes across Asia and Europe. Much of this Mediterranean trade was controlled by Italian merchants, who used their position as middle-men to make enormous profits in western Europe.

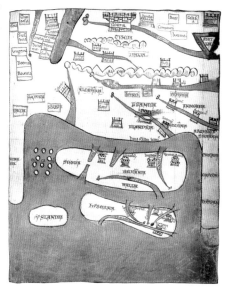

Above: Counting the profits of trade in a Florentine bank. Italian bankers were a frequent sight in Ireland in the thirteenth and early fourteenth centuries. The collapse of Florentine banking houses in the 1340s was one of the many crises afflicting late medieval Europe.

Left: A crude map of western Europe, *c.* 1200 showing Rome (Roma) at the top and Ireland (Hybernia) at the bottom. Limerick, Waterford and Wexford, as well as Dublin, are shown along with the Rivers Liffey, Shannon, Slaney and Suir.

The Fair

The thirteenth century was the time of the great fairs of Latin Christendom (western Europe), the most famous of which were the Champagne fairs in the kingdom of France. Merchants from different lands gathered at the Dublin fair annually for fifteen days in July to trade their goods. Dublin's fair was traditionally held just outside the western city wall on Fair Green.

The right to hold a fair was a valuable privilege. It was granted to the city in 1215 by King John and renewed by Henry III in 1252. The fair began on the eve of a religious festival and the revenue from the first two days of trading was given to the archbishop of Dublin. A charge (custom) was paid to the keeper of the fair on all goods and persons that entered or left the ground. The administration of the fair was a civic duty controlled by the bailiff, his stewards and clerks. Traders were charged a stallage fee for setting up their stalls.

Goods brought to the fair were weighed by the weigh master and inspected for their quality and price. The weigh master ensured that all traders used standard weights and measures. Disputes between traders needed to be settled quickly, before the itinerant vendors moved on. Special fair courts, sometimes known as piepowder courts, dealt with troublemakers and salesmen who breached merchant law. The name 'piepowder' comes from medieval Latin *pede pulverosus*, 'dusty-footed, extended to mean 'travelling peddler' (Modern French *pied poudreux*, 'vagabond'). A small charge called tronage was normally paid to the weigh master, representing his income.

The snacks sold at the fair were prepared by local bakers, whose ovens were located outside the city walls on nearby Cook Street (downhill from Dublinia) to prevent fires from spreading to the main part of the city. The pies may have been filled with minced meat, fruit and spices. Meat fillings may have been rabbit, pork or venison. If you were fasting for religious reasons and could not eat meat, there were local cheeses or dried fish from the quayside of Dublin.

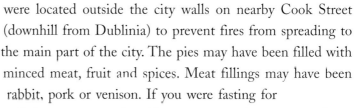

Right: Pie stall.
Far right: Scribe's booth.

Scribes were in great demand at fairs since few people could read or write. For a small fee they would draft or copy grants, wills, private charters and business contracts in Latin

List of stallage fees from the Chain Book

Of every full load of merchandise belonging to one man, two pence.

Of every bale tied up, two pence.

Of every cloth untied, one penny.

Of every butt of wine coming in or going out, two pence.

Of every cut of cloth, one halfpenny.

Of every piece of kitchen-ware, price four pence, one halfpenny.

Of every sack of wool, one halfpenny.

Of every wey of wool, one halfpenny.

Of every piece of linen cloth of five ells more in length than in breadth, one halfpenny.

Of every load of hides, one penny

Of every twenty skins, and upwards, one skin.

Of every otter skin, one penny.

Of every tymbre (i.e. 40) of skins of martens or wolves, two pence.

Of every wey of swine's grease, one penny.

Of every piece of bacon, two pence.

Of every barge-load of merchandise sold by weight, two pence.

Of every ox or cow, two pence.

Of every horse or mare, one penny from the seller and one penny from the buyer.

Of every six hogs, one penny.

Of every six sheep, one penny.

Of every carpet, one halfpenny.

Of every stone of iron, one farthing.

Of every hundred of iron, one penny.

Of every hundred pounds of wax, two pence.

Of every saddle, one halfpenny.

Of every crannoc of salt, one halfpenny.

Of every hundred of kitchen-ware, one penny.

Of every hamper of woad (blue dye) from Vermand, two marks.

Of every hamper of woad from Elbeuf and Amiens, twenty shillings.

Of every hamper of woad from Caen, one mark.

Eight casks make a hamper of every kind of woad.

Below: Halfpennies of the Lord John, *c.* 1190–8 and a Dublin penny of Edward I, *c.* 1295. In 1335 one penny bought 'three little earthenware pots for putting mustard in' for the priory of Holy Trinity.

or other languages. Many scribes were priests and some, known as pardoners, were licensed to sell papal indulgences or pardons. These granted forgiveness in advance for sins, but they were expensive.

The fair was more than just a business event; it was also a gala where people from all walks of life got together to enjoy the sights and sounds. The inns on nearby Winetavern Street (much narrower then than nowadays) would have been busy serving wine to tired travellers. Dancers, jugglers, musicians, acrobats, bears and monkeys performed on Fair Green to the astonished crowds.

Exotic spices were imported from foreign lands, especially by Italian and Flemish merchants. They were valued for their use in preserving food and for the strong and aromatic flavours they gave to elegant dishes. Ready-mixed spices called *poudre douce* (mild) or *poudre fort* (strong) were very popular. Sugar was imported from north Africa and was used very sparingly. The word 'spice' came to be used to describe anything exotic and luxurious, from almonds and figs to perfumes and pigments.

War was never far from the minds of the inhabitants of Dublin who lived under the constant threat of attack. When things were relatively quiet at home, knights made periodic military expeditions, known as Crusades, ostensibly to recover Jerusalem and the Holy Land from the Moslems. Spurs, bits and small weapons were sold locally in Castle Street, but the fair provided an opportunity for locals to see the latest developments in international arms and armour.

One of the most important commodities traded at fairs was cloth. In fact many fairs began with a market selling only cloth. Wool was imported from England while fine silks and damasks were brought in from the east by merchants from Italy. Cloth was measured out by the ell, or more usually by the yard using a stick of a standard length (a yardstick).

Among the Anglo-Normans, blue was probably a common basic colour for clothing; this was made from woad, a dye-plant grown in enormous quantities in Picardy in north-eastern France. An English luxury was scarlet, which was derived from a particular insect. The Irish themselves

From top to bottom: Medicine tent, spicer's stall, armourer's tent and clothing stall.

loved to wear clothes made from colourful textiles, especially robes dyed yellow with saffron. Clothing was fastened using pins, brooches and buckles made from bone or metal. Fashions appear to have varied a good deal across Europe, as we can tell from surviving traditions in national dress.

The great fairs attracted international traders who often needed credit or foreign currency. These and other financial services were provided for merchants by bankers from cities such as Venice and Genoa. Even the term 'bank' came from the Italian word for the bench (*banca*) on which these transactions were done. The currency used in the Dublin fair was the silver penny and halfpenny. Larger sums were reckoned using the shilling, mark and pound, which were all units of account. Smaller transactions were done by barter and exchange of goods.

Top left: Bronze ring-brooch with traces of glass paste in the collets. Found in association with a sill-beam structure during excavations at Back Lane, it is dated by context to the early thirteenth century.

Left: Medieval money: a purse and coins. Money was often carried in a purse attached to the body by a leather belt or thong. It was a natural target for a thief or 'cut-purse'. Coins were usually of silver but occasionally of gold.

Far left: Banking tent.

The Quayside

Ships carrying heavy goods could be loaded and unloaded more easily at a fixed quayside built of timber or stone. During the course of the thirteenth century, as the National Museum of Ireland excavations have shown, a whole succession of quaysides was built farther and farther into the River Liffey at Wood Quay. Immediately to the east of the quay was the slipway where fishermen either sold their catch in their boats or unloaded it for sale in Fishamble Street.

Fishermen drawing in their net. Because of its biblical associations, fishing was regarded as a relatively honourable profession. The city's fishermen were responsible for the float depicting the twelve Apostles in the annual Corpus Christi procession.

Left: Dublin illustration of a ship and a fish (upper left) from the assembly roll of 1456. The River Liffey was a major resource for fish, especially salmon. Some parts of the waterway belonged to the citizens, others to the great churches, and disputes were not uncommon.

Above right: A Dublin illustration of a ship from the assembly roll of 1456. It shows a typical deep-hulled trading vessel with its single mast supported by stays and shrouds and carrying a crow's nest, or observation platform, towards the top.

Right: Reconstruction of a quayside scene at Dublinia. Operating the simple hoist and pulley system would have been demanding work, especially when the tide was low since the distance between the deck and the quayside would have been greater.

Bottom: Thirteenth-century metal fishhooks, one large with surviving leather thong and one small, found close to the waterfront at Wood Quay. Environmental samples suggest that fish were an important food source, and the bones that survive represent a wide variety of species, many of which were caught on a line.

Most merchant ships in the Middle Ages carried a mixed cargo. In Dublin, casks of French wine were unloaded, while bales of hides and fleeces and barrels of salted fish were loaded for the next outward voyage. Sailors and stevedores of different nationalities and speaking a variety of languages worked together. They might expect a visit from one of the city's two water-bailiffs, whose task was to ensure that all incoming seamen, whether from Dublin or from abroad, paid their mooring tax of 2d.

Simple hoists would have been used to raise and lower heavy goods. By the fifteenth century a more elaborate crane and crane-house had been installed at the eastern end of Merchant's Quay, near the bottom of Winetavern Street. This was used in particular for the unloading of casks of wine,

millstones and other materials such as iron (from northern Spain), pitch and resin (from Baltic countries). Special porters were appointed by the city authorities to maintain and operate this device, which depended on human muscle-power. Failure to keep the hoisting rope in good condition would cost them a fine of 6s. 8d. and loss of office.

FINDS BOX

Foreign Trade

Dublin imported many exotic goods through trading links during the Middle Ages, primarily with Britain and France. Jugs came from Bristol, Gloucester and the Bordeaux region. The biggest import into Dublin at this time was French wine, especially from Gascony, so a secondary trade in jugs and goblets grew up around this commodity. During the early medieval period, pottery production was at a minimum in Ireland and alternative materials, such as leather, wood, stone and metals, were in ample supply. After the Anglo-Norman conquest, however, the English and French taste for pottery vessels took off and new trade routes were opened up. The local production of pottery resumed on a much larger scale using new techniques and materials to meet the demand.

The official currency in Dublin during the Middle Ages was the penny, a small silver coin that could be cut in half to make two halfpennies, or into quarters to make four farthings. Even a farthing was quite valuable and too large to use for small transactions, such as buying a drink. For this reason, the inns made their own, unofficial currency known as tavern tokens. These were small stamped coins made of pewter and decorated with a simple design, each representing a different inn or wine-tavern. A hoard of over 2,000 tavern tokens, in a small French pottery money-box, was recovered during excavations at Winetavern Street.

Above: Glazed green wine jug from Saintonge, south-western France.

Far left: Dublin farthings of Edward IV, *c.* 1463. By the late Middle Ages farthings were struck as coins in their own right.

Left: Pewter tokens found in a timber-lined rubbish pit at Winetavern Street. They are of late thirteenth-century English manufacture. Each token is stamped with a simple figural design on one side – for example, a deer wounded by an arrow, a pilgrim with a staff, an ape with an apple – and an armorial device on the other.

Life at Sea

Despite the hazards, including piracy, travel by sea and by navigable waterways was generally easier than journeying overland in the Middle Ages. Though ships got bigger, they were very small by modern standards and at the beginning of this period the steering oar (on the starboard side) was still in use.

By the thirteenth century the standard type of cargo ship in northern Europe was the cog (from the Flemish *kaag*), a sturdy, deep-hulled vessel with one central mast and a sternpost rudder. Some cogs had a 'castle' fore and aft, forming fighting platforms for crossbowmen. These ships were steadily increasing in size; the main reason why land was reclaimed from the River Liffey was to provide a deeper berthage for these bigger ships. In the mid thirteenth century few cogs weighed as much as 100 tonnes, whereas by 1400 their *average* size was around this mark.

Though canvas awnings offered some protection, most of the ship was open to the elements and life on board would have been harsh. The captain was often the owner or part-owner of both the ship and some of the freight. He was responsible for the ship when in port, for ensuring that there was enough food and drink on board, and for the hire and discipline of the crew. Crewmen such as Walter the Steersman who features on the Guild Merchant roll were recruited from many different nationalities and had to take an oath of loyalty to the captain. Punishments usually took the form of fines, but physical methods such as lashing were used as well.

Above left: Marginal sketch of Walter the Steersman on the Guild Merchant roll, occurring at 1226–7. After the captain, the steersman was the most important man on the ship. A hooded garment would have been essential for warmth at sea in open boats and ships.

Above right: An older type of ship fitted with a steering oar. Because the steering oar was always fitted to the right-hand (starboard, from steering board) side of a ship, it was standard practice to moor the vessel on its left-hand, or port, side.

Right: Pirates (on the left) attacking a merchant ship with an impressive array of weapons: arrows, swords and cudgels. One of the pirates is shown standing on a forecastle, or fighting platform, with which many ships of this period were equipped.

FINDS BOX

Ships' Timbers

Ships' timbers are commonly found on urban excavations, often having been re-used, or as a result of dredging operations in the bay. The boat and ship timbers from medieval Dublin range in date from the tenth century (the Fishamble Street site) to the mid thirteenth century (the Wood Quay site). By the twelfth century, Dublin had become a major commercial centre, especially in overseas trade with Bristol, Chester and certain Welsh ports. Dublin was also a location for shipbuilding throughout the period. By the early thirteenth century, seafaring was so vital to Dublin that when King Henry III authorised the mayor and city council to have a common seal in 1229 they chose to depict a ship on the reverse.

A ship fragment found at Fishamble Street (below) shows the clinker style of shipbuilding (where one plank overlaps another and is held together by clenched nails with organic caulking in between to make it watertight). A timber found at Wood Quay was identified as a spacer for the rigging, known as a parrel rib. The rib is dated according to its archaeological context to *c.* 1180–1200. The large number of ships' timbers found in the Dublin excavations survived only because of the unique preservative qualities of its waterlogged soils.

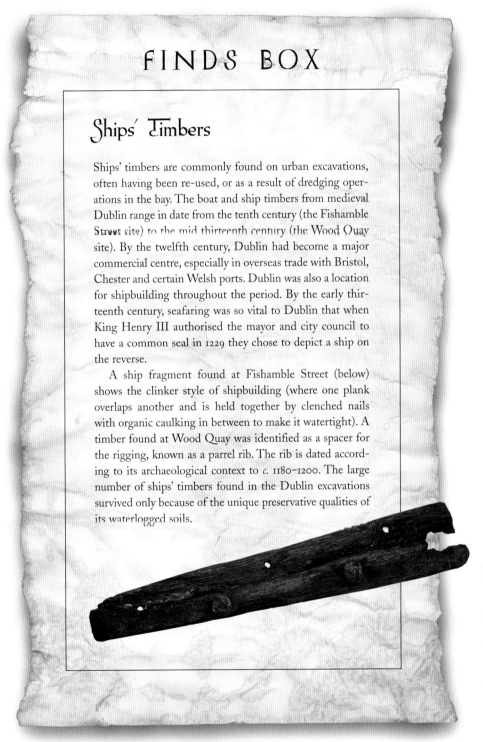

Ships' timbers from Wood Quay and Fishamble Street. Timbers and other nautical artefacts were often re-used in the building of waterfronts, drains and causeways, or discarded as fill behind the quays. They provide important evidence for the maritime history of Dublin.

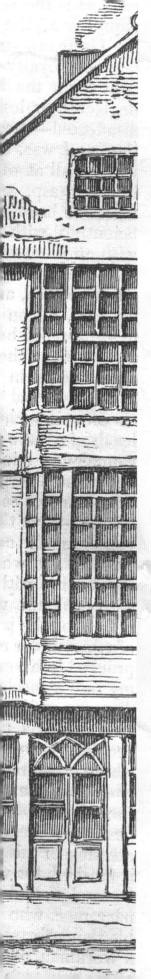

8

Houses and Hygiene

*After 1170 Dublin took on the appearance of
a typical English provincial city and its rulers faced similar
problems relating to the regular supply of fresh water and to
the safe disposal of human and animal waste.*

Thanks to numerous archaeological excavations, we now know a good deal about how Dublin may have looked to its Anglo-Norman and Irish captors in 1170. At that time most houses appear to have had post-and-wattle walls and turf or thatched roofs. They were windowless and smoke from the central hearth would have escaped through a hole in the roof. Even the residences of the Hiberno-Norse kings may have been built in this style, for we are told that a special wattle 'palace' (large hall) was provided for King Henry II and his entourage for their stay in Dublin over the cold winter of 1171–2. Thereafter sturdy, timber-framed houses, some with stone-built ground floors, replaced the older ones and the street-scape probably became more regular. Rocque's map (1756) shows a fairly uniform pattern of building-plots that may have owed a good deal to medieval precedents. A few of the ancient plots still survive in the historic core of the city, but most modern buildings occupy several former plots that have been amalgamated into a single property unit over time.

Town Houses

A typical merchant's or craftworker's house occupied a long, narrow burgage plot. 'Burgage' comes from medieval Latin *burgagium*, referring to a particular type of land tenure. For example, the plot of land was normally held for a money rent rather than in return for labour services and the occupier was free to sublet it or to bequeath it to members of his or her family. As Speed's map suggests and the scale-model shows, houses in medieval Dublin usually had their gables (end walls) on the street frontage, though special arrange-

ments had to be made on corner sites. The garden area behind each house was used for many different purposes: for latrines and rubbish pits, for storage, for keeping animals, and for growing vegetables and fruit.

Town houses varied enormously in size and design. City-centre houses would often have had two or even three storeys above the ground floor and their walls were sometimes built of stone. The basic building material, however, was timber. Heavy timbers were used to construct a rigid framework, the panels being filled in with wattle and daub. Extra space was gained by jettying out the upper floors over the narrow streets. At the other extreme, humble cabins with mud walls probably existed on the outer fringes of the city, many of these being occupied by people of Irish descent.

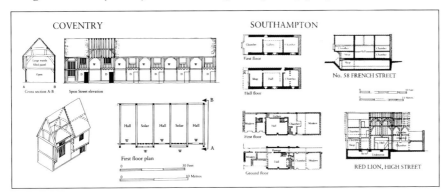

Above left: Grant of a burgage plot to William Russell, 1236, preserved in the White Book. A William Russell was one of the two provosts, or assistants to the mayor, during the mayoral year 1235–6, and they may well have been the same person.

Left: Plans and elevations of English late medieval houses. The style of housing in Dublin was probably similar to that in English cities and towns, but no comparable houses have survived from this period in Ireland. A solar is an upper chamber, usually at first-floor level.

Below: A thirteenth-century rectangular post-and-wattle hut at Back Lane. This structure was probably not used for habitation as it lacked a hearth, but wood chippings found around the entrance suggest an industrial use. Unusually, a stone surface in the foreground comprised several fragments of a rotary quern stone.

Bottom right: Fourteenth- or fifteenth-century floor tiles from St Patrick's Cathedral. Line-impressed tiles such as these appear to have made up a tile pavement 1 metre (3 feet) below floor level, which was covered by the collapse of the nave roof in 1544.

FINDS BOX

Building Evidence

Most of the urban buildings in the Middle Ages would have been constructed from a timber frame and insulated with wattle and daub (wicker-work panels covered with clay or dung). Buildings were roofed using either thatch, slate, stone or earthenware roof-tiles. Medieval masons were commissioned by wealthy patrons to construct magnificent buildings for the display of worldly and spiritual power. The few stone buildings in medieval towns were churches, castles, town halls or strong houses (the latter being owned by wealthy merchants and craftworkers). Glass was expensive and generally used to glaze only stone buildings, so most domestic buildings would have had wooden shutters over the windows to prevent the rain from coming in, and hanging textiles to cut out draughts.

The taste for paving the floors of the finest buildings using decorated, lead-glazed, earthenware tiles was introduced into Ireland some time in the mid thirteenth century and continued until the mid sixteenth century. Although the earliest examples were clearly imported (perhaps from southwest England), a local industry was soon established. These tiles come from the religious sites of medieval Dublin, including both Christ Church and St Patrick's Cathedrals, St Mary's Abbey (located on the north side of the Liffey) and the parish church of St Audoen on High Street. Sadly, hardly any Irish paved floors have survived intact and *in situ*, i.e. in their original location. Two exceptions are known from excavations: St Thomas's Abbey, Meath Market, and the Augustinian friary at Cecilia Street in Temple Bar.

The internal layout of the bigger houses was very varied, but a standard pattern would be a shop at the front on the ground floor with a hall and/or chamber and a kitchen behind; other living and working rooms were located on the first floor, and sleeping and servants' quarters on the upper floor or floors, or in the roof space. Servants, both male and female, were probably a common feature of well-to-do households; as in later centuries, young women in particular would have sought opportunities for personal advancement in a large city such as Dublin. Access to the garden or yard was gained either from a back lane or by means of narrow passage-ways leading at intervals from the street and built over at first-floor level and above. The maximum width of a burgage plot in Dublin was 64 feet (approximately 20 metres).

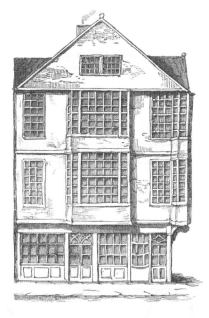

Drawing of the last surviving cage-work house in Dublin, demolished in 1812. This building was probably post-medieval in date, but archaeological evidence suggests that the basic technique of half-timbered construction in Dublin dates back to the thirteenth century.

Inside a Merchant's House

The reconstruction shows two important features of a typical merchant's house – the kitchen below and the office above. At this social level servants were usually employed and a single household might number ten or twelve individuals altogether. This is why population estimates based on the number of recorded heads of household require a higher multiplier for cities and towns than for villages and hamlets. In the early part of our period merchants were often away from home on voyages at sea, leaving their wives in charge, but they gradually became more sedentary and adapted themselves to office life.

Reconstruction of a merchant's house at Dublinia. The merchant pictured on the first floor of the house is clearly removed from the household duties below. He wears brightly coloured clothing reflecting his high social status and stores other clothes in a large chest.

93

Clockwise from top right:
Large well-preserved iron key, showing details of the fine casting work involved in its manufacture. Found at Christchurch Place, it is clearly a high status object. Such a key might have been used to secure the door of a house, or a chest containing valuables.

Iron knife with a bone handle of thirteenth-century date found at Wood Quay. Bone was ideal for manufacturing small functional objects, especially handles, and was a by-product of the medieval diet.

Thirteenth- or fourteenth-century pewter pricket candlestick from High Street. This rare example has an open-work stem with decorative arches on each side of the base. A candle would have been placed on a spike projecting from the circular plate. The form and function of this object attest to the wealth of its owner.

FINDS BOX

Household Fittings

Many household fittings were made from iron, such as large door keys, locks and small hinges. One of the most important household tools was the knife, which had many different uses, from preparing food to carving objects of wood and bone. Medieval eating knives were sharp and well made, often with decorative handles. Most houses would have had a rotary sharpening stone for maintaining the sharpness of knives and other tools with iron blades.

In the Middle Ages, candles were made from beeswax, which was an expensive commodity. Consequently, beeswax candles were used mainly in churches or in the homes of the wealthy. Simpler oil lamps containing wicks lighted most ordinary houses, or tallow and rush candles, which gave off poor light and acrid smoke in poorly ventilated rooms. The main light would have come from the open fire, where all the cooking was done and which would have provided the only source of heat in the house.

Literary texts of a certain genre tell us something of the lifestyle and social standing of merchants' wives. The stock image is that of the Good Wife as mistress of the household. She would manage the servants, treating them fairly but firmly, and setting an example by working alongside them in and around the kitchen. The wife would go to the market for pro-

94

FINDS BOX

Food Preparation

Evidence for the production, preparation and cooking of food and drink in the Middle Ages comes in vessels of many different forms. Grain was stored in large jars to keep it dry and safe from vermin, whereas wine, milk and other liquids were kept in jugs made from local pottery. Mortars (bowls made from strong material) were used for grinding and mixing purposes. Cooking vessels are often blackened with soot where they have been exposed to the flames. As well as pottery, vessels of various types could be made from wood, metal and even stone.

For grinding corn, a rotary quern stone would have been used. Grain was placed between two stones and ground down into coarse flour by the action of the stones as they rubbed together. Grinding corn was the reserved right of private mills, which were driven by rivers within the environs of the medieval city. Payment was required for the use of these mills.

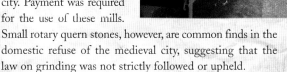

Small rotary quern stones, however, are common finds in the domestic refuse of the medieval city, suggesting that the law on grinding was not strictly followed or upheld.

Far left: Cast skillet, or long-handled saucepan, of thirteenth- or fourteenth-century date. The three legs give the stability for use freestanding over an open fire in the kitchen of a wealthy citizen.

Left: Reconstruction of a merchant's kitchen at Dublinia. On the table there are various jugs and cooking pots containing herbs for flavouring meat and fish dishes, and game hangs from the ceiling. Large joints of meat would have been roasted on a spit over the fire.

Below: Reconstructed wine jug of local manufacture with a green glaze, slashed decoration on the handle and a frilled base. Pottery was being made in Dublin from at least 1190 and probably as early as 1175–80. Potting was a suburban trade located at Crockers' Street, on the line of present-day Oliver Bond Street.

visions and assist with the cooking. From late medieval England a number of recipe collections have survived, such as might have been used in urban households. More delicate tasks, including the making of sweetmeats and conserves from fruit and scented waters from flowers, would have been the wife's business. She, too, might take charge of the kitchen garden, where herbs especially were grown for their flavoursome properties (imported spices being expensive even if her husband traded in them).

Above the kitchen, there might have been an office where the merchant worked, perhaps with the assistance of one of his sons or a trainee clerk. Once a boy was able to add up to 12d. (1s.), he was regarded as having come of age. Merchants would keep a record of their accounts in ledgers. Lists of debts owed by and to merchants appear frequently in their wills. No banks existed in medieval Dublin and money would be stored in a stout box hidden in some part of the house or garden.

Above: A merchant warming himself by the fire. The picture shows some of the features of a rich merchant's house: a partially stone-built interior, a tiled floor, glazed windows and an opulent fireplace. Nevertheless, the furniture is relatively simple.

Water Supply

Being tidal rivers the Liffey and the Poddle were unsuitable either for domestic consumption or for industrial purposes. Before the thirteenth century drinking water would have been carried from some of the smaller watercourses: the Coombe stream (still flowing beneath the roadway) and the Steine (west of St Stephen's Green and Grafton Street) on the south side and the Bradogue (in the present markets' area) on the north side. Dublin's water supply was improved dramatically during the thirteenth century by the construction of the city watercourse from the Poddle, whose flow had been increased by means of an artificial link with the Dodder.

Since the Middle Ages the Poddle has been channelled below ground in brick culverts. Its position is clearly visible where the western end of Dame Street dips noticeably near the Olympia Theatre. The outfall into

Right: Reconstruction of a watermill, discovered by archaeologists, driven by the diverted River Poddle in Patrick Street. Two water channels, one on each side of the street, were built in the late twelfth century as part of an elaborate defensive scheme.

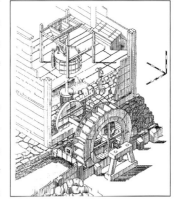

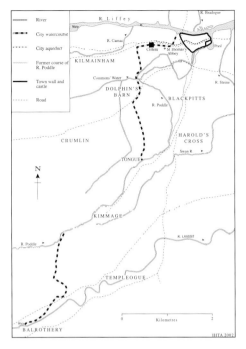

the Liffey through a pipe can still be seen when looking southwards from Lower Ormond Quay.

The new water supply scheme was probably initiated by St Thomas's Abbey to drive its water-mills, which would explain why the water was shared with the citizens in the proportion 2:1 in favour of the monks. The citizens' share was fed to a large cistern near St James's Gate, from which a conduit ran eastwards along the natural ridge towards the castle. Public fountains placed at intervals gave access to this water, but religious houses and prominent individuals were permitted to have their own private supply via small pipes leading from the main conduit. Otherwise women and girls did most of the carrying from the fountains, streams and wells.

The city watercourse in the countryside and parts of the aqueduct running along one side of the streets were open to the elements, and keeping the water clean and uncontaminated was a constant problem. By the second half of the fifteenth century a bannerman (a ceremonial officer) was being appointed regularly at the Michaelmas assembly of the common (enlarged) council. He had the practical responsibility of caring for the city watercourse, seizing animals found grazing there until their owners paid a fine. Polluters were fined as well. A levy of 1d. per shop and 2d. per hall provided an income for the bannerman.

Left: Map showing the water supply system built in the thirteenth century. In the centre is the Tongue, a V-shaped stone device (which still survives) separating the water in the correct proportion between the monks of St Thomas's Abbey and the citizens themselves.

Below: A woman water-carrier. Medieval women had many responsibilities connected with hearth and home. The constant need for fresh water meant hard physical work, but also provided opportunities for social interaction.

Waste Disposal

Medieval towns and cities have a reputation for being unhealthy places to live in and it is probably true that their death-rates were higher than those in the countryside. Nevertheless many regulations for waste disposal were drawn up; the big problem was to ensure compliance. Unlike nowadays, most medieval waste was organic and could be disposed of safely provided that elementary precautions were observed.

English summary of a royal order to clean up Dublin, 1489

The king [Henry VII] has been informed that dung-heaps, swine, pigsties and other nuisances in the streets, lanes and suburbs of Dublin infect the air and produce mortality, fevers and pestilence [plague] throughout the city. Many citizens and sojourners have thus died in Dublin. The fear of pestilence prevents the coming thither of lords, ecclesiastics and lawyers. Great detriments thence arise to his majesty, as well as dangers to his subjects and impediments to his business. The king commands the mayor and bailiffs to cause forthwith the removal of all swine, and to have the streets and lanes freed from ordure, so as to prevent loss of life from pestilential inhalations. The mayor is to expel all vagrants and mendicants from the city.

Human waste was commonly disposed of in cesspits dug in the back gardens of houses, though no doubt some of it found its way into street drains (where these existed). Cesspits could not be sited within 2 feet 6 inches (approximately 0.8 metre) of a neighbour's property. Alternatively some

Cesspit associated with houses at Back Lane. Pits are generally a good source for small finds and also for environmental evidence. Valuable artefacts are sometimes found in the fill of latrines where the original owner decided against their retrieval.

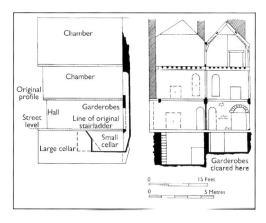

English medieval town houses had built-in lavatories known as garderobes (Modern English 'wardrobes'). We know of at least one public latrine in medieval Dublin; this was situated next to Isolde's Tower (at Lower Exchange Street) and would have discharged directly into the River Liffey.

Animal waste, on the other hand, was a valuable commodity as one of the main sources of fertilizer. There was a public dung-heap beyond Hangman Lane (present-day Hammond Lane) in Oxmantown and presumably others, as one of the tasks of the city constables was to see that the streets were kept free of dung. Carters who brought dung inside the city walls were fined 12d. unless the material was dug into the customer's garden that same day.

As well as dogs, pigs roamed the streets and would have played their part by consuming anything that was edible. Medieval pigs were smaller and more agile than their modern descendants and from time to time a swine-catcher was appointed by the city authorities to impound or kill stray pigs. Butchers and fishmongers were fined if they failed to clean their market stalls, whilst every householder was responsible for cleaning the street outside his own door and was fined 12d. for negligence.

Above left: Garderobe arrangements in a house at Exeter in south western England. Indoor facilities of this kind were probably comparatively rare, since a suitable and efficient outfall, such as a fast-flowing stream or river, was not available to most people.

Left: Composite stone-and-timber pathway at Back Lane of later twelfth- or early thirteenth-century date excavated by Tim Coughlan. The path led from a post-and-wattle house to a cesspit and was made up of unworked, worked and re-used timbers. One of these was L-shaped and may have been part of a ship or the roof of a house.

Far left: Pig eating acorns depicted on a tile from St Patrick's Cathedral. In the countryside pigs were commonly pastured in woodland, where they would feed on acorns, beech-mast, fungi and other forest foods. A special charge called 'pannage' was due to the landowner.

FINDS BOX

Garbage and Knowledge

The thirteenth-century quayside of Dublin was built upon large deposits of refuse and supported by a series of wooden revetments (braced fences) and stone retaining walls. These revetments were built on the edge of the riverbank and rubbish was dumped behind them to reclaim land from the river itself. The result of this activity was to make the river narrower and deeper, enabling ships with deeper draughts to dock.

The material dumped behind the revetments would have been representative of daily life in medieval Dublin, in the same way that a modern city tip is today. The commonest finds during the Wood Quay excavations were animal bones, oyster shells, shards of broken pottery and scraps of wood and leather. More valuable materials, such as precious metals, were generally recycled or kept as souvenirs and so are less well represented in the archaeological record.

The preservative properties in Dublin are rivalled only by sites of about the same period, such as York (England), Trondheim (Norway) and Hedeby/ Haithabu (northern Germany). The rapid deposition of large quantities of material into watery locations at Wood Quay led to anaerobic conditions, i.e. without oxygen, an important element in the process of decay. Organic materials such as leather, wood and textiles, which would have decomposed on a drier site, are thus well preserved.

Wooden revetments at Arran Quay dendro-dated to the early fourteenth century. They were later replaced by a stone wall. Dendrochronology is the study of tree-rings of excavated timbers, preferably oak, to establish the date of a particular site, or feature.

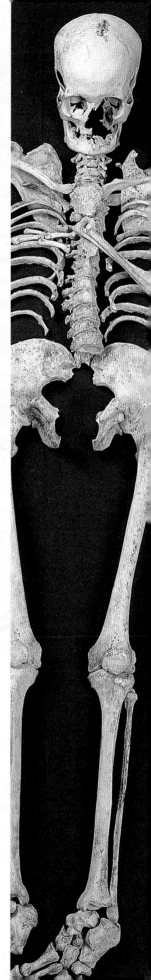

9
Life and Death

Written sources tend to tell us more about well-to-do members of the urban community, whereas archaeology also reveals the ordinary Dubliner, both in life and in death.

Prior to the medical improvements of the nineteenth and twentieth centuries, life expectancy everywhere was much lower than nowadays. The highest rates of loss occurred in infancy and in early childhood (before the age of five), after which prospects for survival improved somewhat. Even so, English coroners' records of accidental deaths show that young people were often scalded fatally by cauldrons containing boiling water. In adulthood men were particularly prone to death (or serious injury) arising from casual violence linked to the universal carrying of knives, while women were always at risk during pregnancy and childbirth. Medieval armies were frequently decimated by dysentery caused by the drinking of contaminated water when on campaign. Drowning was a common reason why a person met with a premature death, for instance by falling down a well or from horseback when crossing a river. It may be assumed, despite the lack of direct evidence, that medieval Dubliners experienced these and other hazards of life in equal measure; the Black Death merely made a bad situation even worse than before.

FINDS BOX

Animals, Hunting and Fishing

Shells, bones and skulls were all recovered from the habitation levels of medieval Dublin. By quantifying the relative amounts of different animal bones from a site, it is possible to assess the typical diet of the inhabitants. In this way, we know that medieval Dubliners ate mostly beef, mutton and pork. The tool marks on domestic animal bones are also an interesting source of information regarding medieval tools and butchery practices. Of course, animals were not only valuable as a source of meat. Sheep were needed for their wool and cattle for dairy products and hides, as well as for pulling carts. Cats were bred for their soft fur during the Middle Ages and they also helped to keep vermin at bay. As today, dogs were kept for hunting, security and as companions.

Among the more unusual animal remains found in Dublin are a wolf skull and a vertebra of a whale. In the Middle Ages, wolves were hunted to such a degree that they are now no longer found in the wild in Ireland, having died out in the eighteenth century. The whale bone was probably imported to Dublin from Scandinavia for use as a luxury raw material for carving fine objects, though whales may also have been hunted or beached off the Irish coast from time to time. Fish and seafood (especially oysters, herring and eel) formed an important part of the medieval diet and fishing was a major part of Dublin's economy. Fish was preserved by air-drying, salting or pickling and was exported to the Continent in large quantities.

Wolf, cat and dog skulls (left to right): Three skulls found in thirteenth-century levels at Wood Quay. According to Anglo-Norman commentator Gerald of Wales, wolves in Ireland had their young as early as December because of the mild climate. He used the wolf as a metaphor for the evils of treachery and plunder', which, he wrote, also blossomed in Ireland 'before their season'.

High Standards of Living

Merchants dominated the city council in the Middle Ages as a result of their leading socio-economic position. Other élite groups lived in the wealthier monasteries, such as St Mary's Abbey (Cistercians), St Thomas's Abbey (Augustinian canons) and Kilmainham Priory (Knights Hospitaller). Another wealthy house was Holy Trinity Priory, which was attached physically and institutionally to Christ Church Cathedral.

The most detailed record to have come down to us from medieval Dublin in relation to standards of living is a seneschal's (a steward or an official) account from Holy Trinity Priory for the years 1337–46. It shows in general that the Augustinian canons who served the cathedral for religious purposes and who lived in the adjacent priory were living a life of considerable luxury on the

Christ Church canons singing mass in the mid fourteenth century. Archbishop John of St Paul (1349–62) was responsible for building the 'long choir' at the cathedral. His main purpose may have been to provide a bigger space for choral singing.

eve of the Black Death. Most of their food came from three home farms, at Deansgrange, Glasnevin and Grangegorman. The prior himself had his own dining table (costing 6s. 1d. when new) and he entertained important visitors in royal style.

Bread was eaten with every meal, either baked in the priory's bakehouse or bought outside in the city. Prepared dishes such as pies and pastries were often purchased in nearby Cook Street. Even breakfast was a substantial meal, consisting of bread, capons (castrated cocks), pastries, oysters, salmon, wine or ale. Dinner and supper often featured three types of meat or, on Fridays and during Lent, three types of fish. Eels and oysters were commonly eaten as well. Fruit and vegetables receive less attention on the account roll, but a limited range would have been available. Various herbs and spices were used for flavouring food, especially ginger, mustard, pepper and saffron.

Clockwise from top right:
Single-sided, thirteenth-century, polished antler comb found at Wood Quay. Combs were of composite construction, and copper rivets held saw-cut teeth plates and decorated side plates together. Hundreds of combs and their manufacturing waste have been found in Dublin, suggesting they were mass-produced in zoned workshops.

Thirteenth-century shoe found at Wood Quay. Excavations at nearby High Street, where the majority of leather workshops were located, revealed a thick layer of fragments of worked leather, including over a thousand worn soles of boots and shoes.

Thirteenth-century ring brooches from Wood Quay. Such brooches were commonly used to fasten the slit at the neck of the kirtle or gown, or to fasten a cloak or mantle over the breast. The pins on both these brooches are slightly bent, probably owing to the weight of the cloth they were holding.

Fifteenth-century buckle and plate ornamented with an embossed griffin from Nicholas Street. In the Middle Ages every man wore a belt from which he suspended a knife and sometimes a sword. A buckle like this would have been a mark of the wearer's wealth.

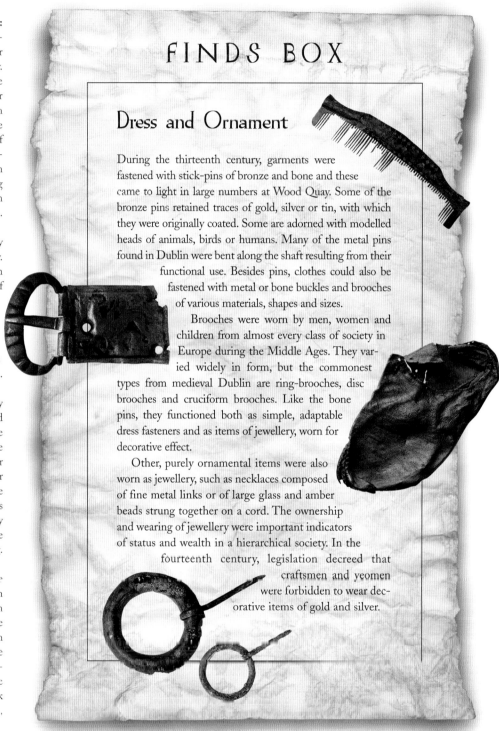

FINDS BOX

Dress and Ornament

During the thirteenth century, garments were fastened with stick-pins of bronze and bone and these came to light in large numbers at Wood Quay. Some of the bronze pins retained traces of gold, silver or tin, with which they were originally coated. Some are adorned with modelled heads of animals, birds or humans. Many of the metal pins found in Dublin were bent along the shaft resulting from their functional use. Besides pins, clothes could also be fastened with metal or bone buckles and brooches of various materials, shapes and sizes.

Brooches were worn by men, women and children from almost every class of society in Europe during the Middle Ages. They varied widely in form, but the commonest types from medieval Dublin are ring-brooches, disc brooches and cruciform brooches. Like the bone pins, they functioned both as simple, adaptable dress fasteners and as items of jewellery, worn for decorative effect.

Other, purely ornamental items were also worn as jewellery, such as necklaces composed of fine metal links or of large glass and amber beads strung together on a cord. The ownership and wearing of jewellery were important indicators of status and wealth in a hierarchical society. In the fourteenth century, legislation decreed that craftsmen and yeomen were forbidden to wear decorative items of gold and silver.

FINDS BOX

Games and Music

Medieval life was far more labour-intensive than life today because most jobs had to be done by hand. By dusk, most people were ready to retire to their beds after their evening meal. Holy days were often times for festivities and celebration, providing a balance between work and leisure. But how did people amuse and entertain themselves during their free time? During the Middle Ages, most of the population of Europe would have been illiterate. In the absence of the written word, storytelling was an important aspect of everyday life, serving a dual purpose by keeping local history and folklore alive, whilst at the same time acting as a form of entertainment. Other communal forms of entertainment, such as singing and dancing, served an important social function, but they are archaeologically invisible.

Additional activities that occupied the leisure time of people in the Middle Ages included playing board games and musical instruments. Although archaeological remains of this type are regrettably few, excavations in Dublin have revealed some evidence for both pursuits. Musical instruments found in Dublin include whistles made of animal bone and wood. Disc-shaped gaming pieces of antler are also in evidence, as are pegged examples, made of wood or bone, for use with a perforated game-board. A small stone found during excavations at Wood Quay bears scratch marks for an impromptu game of nine men's morris, which was actually a game called 'merels' played with counters by two persons. Only a few medieval dice of bone and ivory are marked out as they would be today, i.e. so that the numbers on opposing faces always total seven.

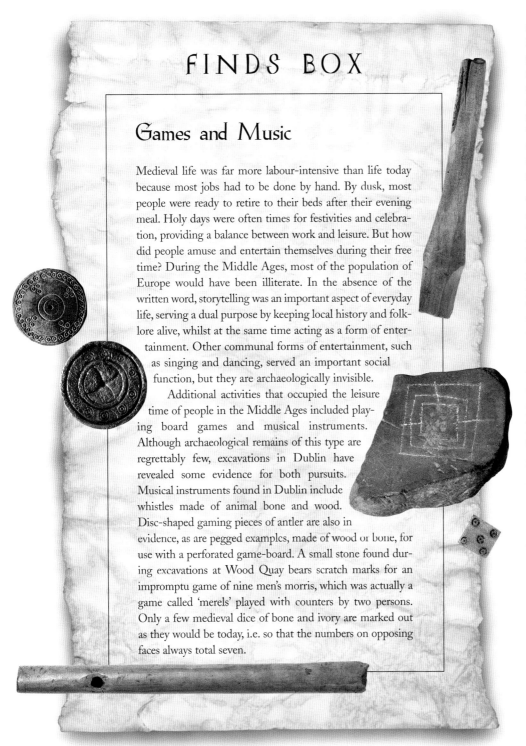

Clockwise from left:
Disc-shaped bone gaming pieces of Anglo-Norman type. Although they resembled draughts, such counters were probably used in a game known as 'tables' played with two or three dice. Draughts did not become popular until after 1500.

Thirteenth-century wooden harp peg from Wood Quay. The Anglo-Norman commentator, Gerald of Wales, remarked on the incomparable musical skill of the Irish people, especially with the harp and tympanum (early drum).

Stone game board from Wood Quay. The game of merels or nine men's morris was popular in the Middle Ages. It could be played on a simple game board, or a grid scratched into the ground. The purpose of the game is to get three counters (stones or wooden balls) in a straight row.

Thirteenth-century bone die from Wood Quay, for use in games of chance. The numbers are represented by dots ringed by small circles. The die is not numbered in the orthodox fashion.

Thirteenth-century whistle from Winetavern Street with a blowhole but no finger holes.

Life Expectancy

In the Middle Ages death was so commonplace that it could be joked about. Even before the Black Death the average life expectancy may have been as low as 30 to 35 years: high infant mortality and the risks of child-birth are among the many reasons for this low figure. Personal hygiene was of a poor standard mainly because of the difficulty of heating water in large quantities. Most people suffered from lice, despite the flea-traps worn on the body; these were small, funnel-shaped devices containing a sticky sub-stance. Many towns had public bath-houses and those that admitted both sexes generally got a bad reputation!

Medicine at this time combined classical knowledge with alchemy, astrology, fortune telling and traditional herbal cures. Illnesses were thought to have been caused by imbalances in the body's four main fluids or humours. If you had too much blood it could be balanced by bloodlet-ting. If you needed teeth pulling, or surgery, but could not afford to pay the real doctor, you would visit the barber-surgeon. These amateur surgeons were usually barbers or even butchers and any skill that they possessed was probably of the folkloric sort. A white pole with a red rag wrapped around it represented the blood and bandages of their trade.

The worst illness of all was leprosy, for which there was no cure and which led to social exclusion. Lepers had to carry a clapper or bell to announce their presence. Some doctors wore special hoods stuffed with

A mock funeral procession of dogs and hares. Even townspeople lived in close proximity to a wide variety of animals, which provided a fund of folk-tales and moral lessons. Dogs and hares – traditional enemies – here cheat death together.

herbs to protect themselves from such pestilence. Like many cities and large towns, Dublin had its own leper 'hospital', referred to in 1230 as 'the leper-house of St Stephen'. It had been founded as a charitable institution before

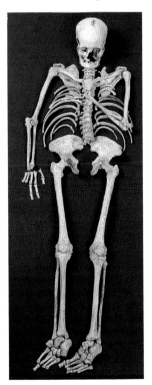

1192 and was eventually taken over by the city authorities. St Stephen's Hospital is shown as three separate houses on Speed's map, though only the adjacent church is named in the key (no. 19).

Medical knowledge was mainly unscientific. Nevertheless some traditional methods were sensible enough: for example, the practice of using women's breast-milk as a solvent on which to base ointments. A major limitation was the lack of anatomical research, which was discouraged by the Church because of the belief in resurrection. Thus ignorance persisted: for example, the notion of the stomach as a cauldron in which food was cooked by heat from the liver. In addition surgery was attempted without the benefit of effective anaesthetics.

Above: Preparation of medicines. All kinds of dry ingredients were experimented with for their medicinal potential, a small number of which may actually have been beneficial to patients. In addition plants provided effective remedies for certain conditions, a fact that is still recognised today.

Below left: Twelfth-century female skeleton discovered at Wood Quay. (see also pp108–10). The position of each burial in an archaeological excavation is recorded on a special feature sheet and photographed from above. This enables the bones to be re-articulated for display and may tell us something about the cause of death.

FINDS BOX

A Medieval Dubliner

During the campaign of excavations carried out by Dr Patrick Wallace of the National Museum of Ireland, at Wood Quay, a skeleton was found on the old south bank of the Liffey, just below Christ Church Cathedral. The adult skeleton was discovered in a shallow trench cut into the estuarine mud along with the remains of two small children aged between three and five. The bones have now been articulated in order to recreate as closely as possible the position in which they were discovered. The triple burial was less than a metre (3 feet) to the south of a larger mass grave that contained the remains of at least five individuals. The fact that these people were buried in unconsecrated ground suggests that they may have been social outcasts in some way – perhaps criminals, prisoners of war or victims of an epidemic.

According to osteoarchaeologists, the skeleton is that of a female aged between 35 and 45 years. Despite having been interred for approximately nine centuries, the bones were reasonably well preserved. Measurements taken from the long bones indicate that the woman stood about 1.58 metre (5 feet 2 inches) tall. The bones do not offer any clue as to the cause of death, although this does not rule out a violent end, as mortal wounds may have been limited to the soft tissue. In life, ▶

Skull of twelfth-century female skeleton found in the Christ Church area. Osteoarchaeologists study the bones of a skeleton to determine its sex, age at death, build and appearance. The manner in which the body was buried also provides information about religion and beliefs.

Christian burials of the period are usually simple graves in a formal enclosure with the body oriented east-west. Grave goods are rare although archaeologists sometimes find traces of wooden coffins, shroud pins or textile fragments.

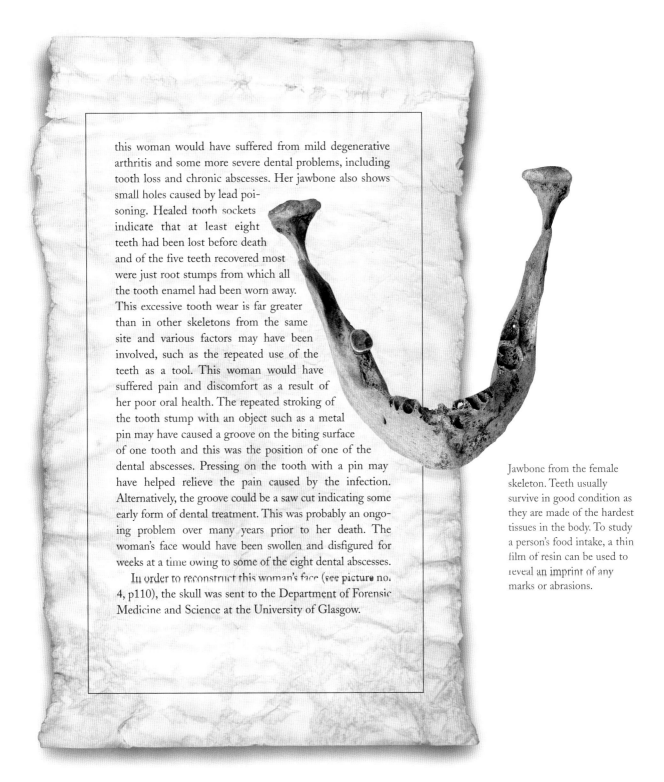

this woman would have suffered from mild degenerative arthritis and some more severe dental problems, including tooth loss and chronic abscesses. Her jawbone also shows small holes caused by lead poisoning. Healed tooth sockets indicate that at least eight teeth had been lost before death and of the five teeth recovered most were just root stumps from which all the tooth enamel had been worn away. This excessive tooth wear is far greater than in other skeletons from the same site and various factors may have been involved, such as the repeated use of the teeth as a tool. This woman would have suffered pain and discomfort as a result of her poor oral health. The repeated stroking of the tooth stump with an object such as a metal pin may have caused a groove on the biting surface of one tooth and this was the position of one of the dental abscesses. Pressing on the tooth with a pin may have helped relieve the pain caused by the infection. Alternatively, the groove could be a saw cut indicating some early form of dental treatment. This was probably an ongoing problem over many years prior to her death. The woman's face would have been swollen and disfigured for weeks at a time owing to some of the eight dental abscesses.

In order to reconstruct this woman's face (see picture no. 4, p110), the skull was sent to the Department of Forensic Medicine and Science at the University of Glasgow.

Jawbone from the female skeleton. Teeth usually survive in good condition as they are made of the hardest tissues in the body. To study a person's food intake, a thin film of resin can be used to reveal an imprint of any marks or abrasions.

Facial Reconstruction

After preparation to fill in missing sections of bone (1), details of the skull were fed into a computer via an optical laser scanning system. Facial reconstruction using 3D computer programmes is a routine procedure as an aid to victim identification in police forensic cases as well as for archaeological and historical interest. Previous historical subjects have included Robert the Bruce, the 'Tyrolean Iceman' and an Egyptian mummy. A computer programme adds muscle and tissue to the skull appropriate to the age and sex of the subject. Soft parts of the face such as the ears, lips, around the eye sockets and much of the nose leave no hard, skeletal remains and can only be suggested. Finally, the computer stretches a suitable 'skin' over the results and the skull's probable facial characteristics can be viewed from any angle (2). The pictures produced by the computer are taken a step further by employing the skills of trained portrait painters and sculptors to humanise the computer's prediction. In this instance the sculptor was already experienced in this type of work, having previously worked on the facial reconstruction of Viking skeletons from York in England (3).

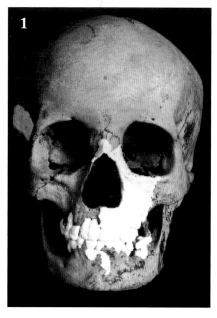

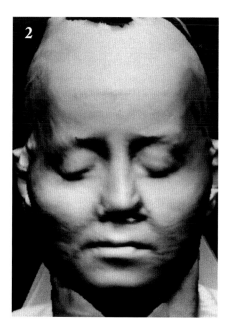

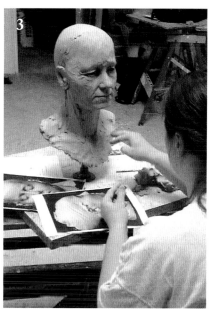

Last Will and Testament

As their wills and houses testify, merchants were among the wealthiest members of the urban community and tended therefore to wield political influence as well. One of the best ways to understand the lifestyle of medieval merchants is to study their wills. Merchants formed the main body of leading citizens in Dublin, as in most towns of this period. Many traded in a wide variety of goods, whereas some were specialists.

For Dublin the main source is the register of wills and inventories drawn up in the time of Archbishops Michael Tregury and John Walton (1457–83). This manuscript still survives in the library of Trinity College and its leaves consist of the relatively novel material, paper, rather than the more traditional parchment.

Among the customary laws of Dublin was one to the effect that, within a year and a day of a testator's death, a will that disposed of property within the city and its liberty should be shown to the mayor and the two bailiffs, and read out at the High Cross on three market days. Twelve citizens would investigate the rightful ownership of the property and a copy of the will would be lodged with the city's own records.

Some of the Dublin merchants whose wills have survived owned property in the county as well as in the city, and sometimes elsewhere in Ireland and even in England. A few carried on farming in addition to trading in items such as cloth, yarn, animal skins, leather, iron, salt, alum, tin, pitch and resin. Others practised as gold- and silver-smiths and most acted as money-lenders, hence the lists of articles held in pledge with them at the time of death. Not infrequently a wife is described as joint owner with her late husband.

We do not know what caused the death of the Dublin merchant, Peter Higley. He lived in the parish of St Michael the Archangel and seems to have dealt mainly in hardware, as is suggested by the details given at the beginning of the inventory of his goods. The document is dated 28 October 1476 and he was to be buried in Christ Church Cathedral, where his son John was a canon.

Above: Effigy of Archbishop Michael Tregury (1449–71) in St Patrick's Cathedral. Tregury was a Cornishman and the emblem of St Michael, above his right hand, is reminiscent of the pilgrimage site of St Michael's Mount, near Penzance in the far south-west of England.

Extracts from the inventory and will of Peter Higley

Inventory of all the goods of Peter Higley, citizen of Dublin, Millany, his wife, and their children, made the 28th day of the month of October, in the year of our Lord 1476.

First, they have in salt 16 weys worth £32.

Item, two tons of iron worth £9 6s. 8d.

Item, 4 dakers and 2 hides of leather worth 42s.

Item, in pitch and resin worth 13s. 4d.

Item, in merchandise in the shop worth 100s.

Item, in vessels of brass, lead and pewter, and other household utensils, worth £10 13s. 4d.

Item, in grain in the barn worth 20 marks.

Item, 9 acres of wheat and barley, sown in the field, worth 45s.

Item, 9 cows worth 30s.

Item, 3 oxen worth 24s.

Item, 13 calves worth 21s. 8d.

Item, 7 pigs worth 3s. 4d.

Item, 4 pairs of wheels, with their belongings, and wagons, worth 30s.

Item, 3 ploughs, with their iron and other belongings, worth 5s.

Item, 7 cart-horses worth 40s.

Item, a horse worth 10s.

Item, 50 sheep young and old worth 20s.

Item, in boards and laths, with other necessaries for building, worth 20s.

Sum of the goods £85 11s.

These are the debts which [are due] to them.

First, David Purcell, of Dublin, merchant, owes £17.

Item, other debtors are bound to them in £40 of silver, as in the book of shop debts is more fully contained.

Sum of the debts which are due to them £57.

These are the debts which they owe.

First, to the lord deputy and chancellor 33s. 4d.

Item, for divers rents £6.

Item, to their servants 30s.

Item, to Thomas Laundey, chaplain, 13s. 4d.

Sum of the debts which they owe £9 16s. 8d.

Clear sum £132 14s. 8d.

Portion of the deceased £44 4s. 8d.

In the name of God. Amen. I, the aforesaid Peter Higley, sound in mind though weak in body, do make my testament in this manner.

> First, I bequeath my soul to Almighty God, the Blessed Virgin Mary, and all the saints, and my body to be buried in the chapel of St Mary the Virgin, in the cathedral church of the Holy Trinity, Dublin [Christ Church].
>
> Item, I leave the residue of the term which I hold in and of 40 acres of land near Killeigh from the baron of Skreen, and the third part of all common goods acquired between us to Millany, my wife, during her life.
>
> Item, I leave to Patrick and Thomas, my sons, and Agnes, my daughter, the third part of my goods appertaining to them, and I will that the said third part remain in the hands of Robert Chillame, of Dublin, until they arrive at legal age.
>
> Item, I leave 20s. to the church of the Holy Trinity, Dublin, to be taken out of the rent of the house in which Henry Barbor lives, in St Patrick's Street.
>
> Item, I leave to my parish church of St Michael [the Archangel], Dublin, 20s.
>
> Item, I leave to each order of mendicant friars of the city of Dublin 6s. 8d.
>
> Item, I leave to John Ward 20s. and a russet gown.
>
> Item, I leave to Joan Alleyn, towards her marriage, 6s. 8d.
>
> Item, I leave to Brother John Higley, canon regular of the said cathedral church of the Holy Trinity, my son, 13s. 4d. during his life, to be taken yearly out of the rent of the houses belonging to me in St Patrick's Street, after the said cathedral church shall have been satisfied of the said 20s. by me as above bequeathed.
>
> Item, I leave to Thomas Higley, my son, all the messuages, lands, tenements, rents and services, with their appurtenances, which I have in St Patrick's Street and in New Street …

And of this my testament I make, ordain and constitute the said Robert Chillame and my son, Brother John Higley, already mentioned, executors, to perform and dispose for the health of my soul, as to them may seem most expedient. But I will that all my other goods, be they in kind or in the hands of debtors, not specially mentioned in this testament, be distributed for the health of my soul, and that satisfaction be made to my creditors by the hands of the said executors.

10

Religion

*Religion played a very important part
in the life of medieval Dubliners, as the number of parish
churches and monasteries indicates.*

During the Middle Ages most of western Europe belonged to the Roman Church with the pope as its supreme ruler. Within the greater body of the organised Church, the fundamental distinctions were between the clergy and the laity (the latter being the Christian faithful) and between the 'regular' clergy (monks and nuns following a monastic rule) and the 'secular' clergy (archbishops, bishops, priests, etc. ministering to the faithful). The pattern of churches and religious houses reflected these distinctions, as well as the extraordinary diversity and richness of Christian culture. In the thirteenth century the friars came to Dublin – in chronological order the Dominicans, Franciscans, Friars of the Sack, Carmelites and Augustinians – who lived in convents scattered around the suburbs and who begged for alms in the streets. Friars were a more visible Christian presence than members of the enclosed orders, especially since some of them became expert preachers. The Christian message was now more available to ordinary citizens but, ironically, the perceived gulf between what was preached and what was practised became a source of dissatisfaction for at least some of the laity.

Parish Churches

Big towns and cities in the Middle Ages tended to have several parish churches and sometimes a very large number of them. Dublin was unusual in that there were more parish churches outside the walls than inside them, along with an impressive range of monastic foundations. Like those in the surrounding countryside, urban parish churches were often small in size and simple in layout.

GRANGE CHURCH

BALDONGAN

ST. MARY'S CHURCH, HOWTH

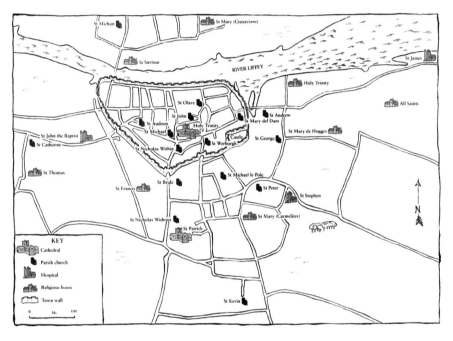

Above left: Map of the churches, religious houses and hospitals. The distribution of these buildings reflects the size and importance of the four suburbs. Monasteries occupied a great deal of space and were usually located outside the defensive walls and inside their own enclosures.

Above right: Ground plans of rural parish churches in the Dublin region. Most surviving country churches have a very basic plan, often without any major distinction between the nave and chancel. The only surviving urban example from the city, St Audoen's, had an unusually complex design.

The dedications of the parish churches inside the walls reflect the diverse origins of the city's medieval population: St Audoen (Anglo-Norman, in Cornmarket), St Olave (Norse, in Fishamble Street) and St Werburgh (English, in Werburgh Street). St Audoen's was by far the biggest of the parish churches inside the main walled enclosure and its parish included much of the land reclaimed from the River Liffey in the thirteenth century. No new parish church was provided for residents of the riverside district beyond the original north wall.

The extensive suburbs had larger parishes, though the population density was probably lower, especially after the Black Death epidemic of 1348. One

St Audoen's Church viewed from the west. There are six bells in the tower, of which three are the oldest in the city. They were cast either in Bristol or in York in 1423 and each has its own dedication.

unusual circumstance is that there never was a separate building for the church of St Nicholas Without (*with-out or outside* the city walls); instead the north transept of St Patrick's Cathedral was walled off to serve as a parish church. A special feature of the church of St Michael le Pole was the round tower dating probably from *c.* 1100 and which survived down to the late eighteenth century. Its parish, however, is described as depopulated and impoverished in the middle of the sixteenth century, when it was annexed to that of St Werburgh's Church.

St Michael's Church

The former Synod Hall of the Church of Ireland, which houses the Dublinia exhibition, stands on the site of the medieval parish church of St Michael the Archangel, the patron saint of mariners and others. This church is first mentioned *c.* 1178, but its origins appear to go back further as a dependent chapel of Christ Church Cathedral. St Michael's later acquired the status of a parish church. It was completely rebuilt in the 1670s, though only the tower now survives.

Portrait of St Michael the Archangel (middle figure). St Michael was the only archangel to have a feast-day in the calendar of Latin Christendom. Michaelmas (29 September) was universally used for making customary payments after harvest time, including Dublin's city rent (fee farm).

The medieval parish of St Michael's was almost the smallest in the city, comprising an area of between 2.0 and 2.4 hectares (5 and 6 acres). Rocque's map of Dublin (1756) shows the rebuilt

Left: Effigy of a priest or deacon in St Patrick's Cathedral, thirteenth century. Made of fine-grained crystalline limestone, though badly repaired with cement, it can be seen in the south choir aisle. His hair is shown in small curls and he is apparently tonsured.

Below: St Michael and the serpent, representing Satan. On the basis of Revelations, St Michael was honoured as the 'captain of the heavenly host', and the protector of Christians in general and of soldiers in particular. Their greatest enemy, of course, was Satan.

church on what was presumably its medieval site, with a small burial ground to the north. The south wall of the church fronted on to High Street and we know that the fresh-water aqueduct ran just outside this wall on its way to the castle. There is a tradition that there were wooden figures of St Michael and Satan on the exterior of the east end of the church before the Reformation. In that case the houses shown by Rocque would not have existed in the Middle Ages.

FINDS BOX

Religious Belief

During the Middle Ages religion played a central role in most people's life and death. Pious people of all ages and from all walks of life undertook journeys to holy places, known as pilgrimages. In Ireland, Lough Derg and Croagh Patrick were the great centres of pilgrimage. In England, the most famous shrine was that of St Thomas Becket at Canterbury, which was the focus of Chaucer's *Canterbury Tales*. Pilgrimages to distant lands were time-consuming, expensive and dangerous.

Like tourists today, those who embarked on such journeys often acquired souvenirs (pilgrim badges and ampullae or small, ornate vessels with two handles) at each place they visited. These souvenirs were mostly made of lead alloy and were decorated with iconography relating to the saint or martyr of the shrine. Ampullae were designed as cheap containers for healing waters, which were a feature of many pilgrim resorts.

In the Middle Ages, it was believed by many that relics had the power to effect miraculous cures. These secondary uses generally proved to be quite profitable for the churches that owned important relics, leading to an illicit trade in the sale of false relics. Relics could either be parts of the bodies of holy persons, for example, the remains of St Lachtin's Arm, or they might be objects associated with the holy life of a saint, such as St Patrick's Bell.

Right: Replica of a lead-alloy ampulla (holy water flask) from England. The Latin inscription reads 'In honour of St Wulfstan' and refers to a saint who had been the bishop of Worcester in the eleventh century. A picture of Wulfstan is visible on the front.

Far right: Reliquary of the heart of St Laurence O'Toole in Christ Church Cathedral. Archbishop of Dublin from 1162 to 1180 and founder of Holy Trinity Priory, he died in Normandy while on his way to Rome and his heart was brought back to Dublin.

In the early fifteenth century the Shoemakers' Guild founded a chantry in the chapel of the Blessed Virgin Mary inside St Michael's Church. Chantries, a characteristic form of late medieval Christian devotion, were financed with the aim of providing one or more priests to sing (French *chanter*) daily mass for the souls of the founder(s) or other specified individuals and it was common for a particular chapel to be allocated for this purpose. Chantries were founded both by private individuals and by corporate bodies such as craft guilds.

The Reformation

The Lambert Simnel episode proved to be a political misjudgement on the part of the leading citizens, who were forced to make their peace with the new king of England, Henry VII. Nearly half a century later, however, by their opposition to the aristocratic rebel, Silken Thomas, the Dubliners ingratiated themselves with the next Tudor king, Henry VIII. The murder of Archbishop John Alen by supporters of Silken Thomas in 1534 and the appointment by Henry VIII of a reforming successor, George Browne, brought the Reformation to the city in a particularly dramatic way.

Christ Church Cathedral from the south in 1826, showing the late fourteenth-century long choir. The pre-restoration cathedral looked very different from its heavily-restored successor. The upper part of the tower was rebuilt with clock faces in *c.* 1600.

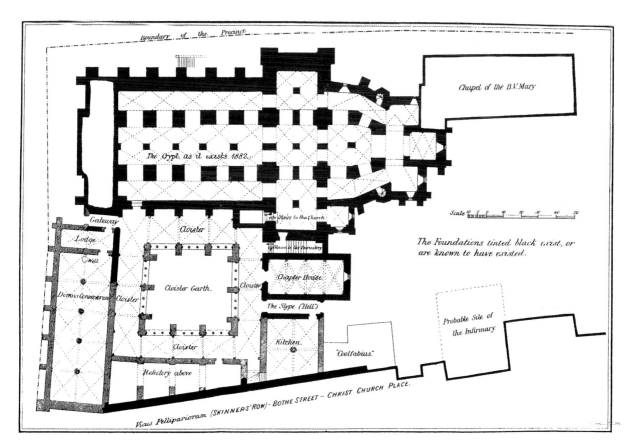

Boundary of the Precinct

Chapel of the B.V. Mary

The Crypt as it exists 1882.

Scale

The Foundations tinted black exist, or are known to have existed.

Gateway

Lodge

Well

Cloister

Cloister

Domus Conversorum

Cloister

Cloister Garth.

Cloister

with Stairs to the Church

Stairs to the Dormitory

Chapter House.

Probable Site of the Infirmary

The Slype (Hell)

Cloister

Kitchen.

"Coolfabius."

Refectory above

Vicus Pelliparioram (SKINNERS' ROW) - BOTHE STREET - CHRIST CHURCH PLACE.

Above: Plan of Holy Trinity Priory in relation to the crypt of Christ Church Cathedral. The priory buildings were located on the southern, sunny side of the cathedral. The cloister walk gave access to various doorways and shelter to monks reading and writing in good natural light.

Right: James Simon's drawing of the High Cross of Dublin, 1794. The cross at the city centre was four-sided and about 5 metres (16-18 feet) tall. The decorative panels appear to have been biblical and heraldic, while the orb on top represented universality.

One part of Archbishop Browne's task, as happened in England and Wales, was to confiscate the jewels and precious metals that adorned statues and shrines. In addition to this, and after some hesitation, the new archbishop ordered the destruction of all sacred relics in his archdiocese. Those of Christ Church Cathedral and its adjoining priory were laid out in a heap in Skinners' Row not far from the High Cross and burnt in 1538. Some of them may have escaped destruction, however, including the most precious of all, the Bacall Íosa or Staff of Jesus, which was believed to have been given to St Patrick himself.

Despite the Reformation, the people of Dublin continued to enjoy their religious festivals or holy days, from which we get the word 'holidays'. One of the most important of these days was the feast of Corpus Christi, when the population of Dublin turned out to see an enormous pageant. Great carts were decorated, each by a particular guild of the city, upon which appropriate scenes of the Bible were acted

out for the crowd. The mariners and shipbuilders, for example, performed Noah and the Ark, the shoemakers Cain and Abel, and the glovers Adam and Eve.

By the end of 1540, all of the city's religious houses and hospitals had been closed down on the orders of the English government. The fate of their buildings was determined by their value and potential for re-use. Most of the churches themselves were demolished, but ancillary buildings were more adaptable and some of these survived for a considerable period of time. Nevertheless the coming of the Reformation was a decisive stage in the ruination of the medieval city and the year 1540 is a fitting point at which to complete our story.

Gabriel Beranger's sketch of the tower of St John's Hospital, *c.* 1770. Because it was run on religious lines, St John the Baptist's Hospital, outside Newgate, was dissolved in 1539. It continued to operate on a smaller scale as a charitable institution for poor male residents.

The Rediscovery and Recreation of Medieval Dublin

As we have already seen, Speed's map of Dublin as it was in the year 1610 shows the late medieval city remarkably intact, apart from its monasteries and hospitals. Even for some of these, substantial remains still survived. From the late seventeenth century onwards, however, the city expanded rapidly and the historic core was largely redeveloped or allowed to decay further. A dramatic start to these processes was a major accidental fire at the castle in 1684.

The first signs of an interest in rediscovering the medieval city in a scientific way date back to the 1840s, the time of the Great Famine in Ireland. Viking burials began to be found at Kilmainham and Islandbridge in the course of rail-

View of Christ Church Cathedral from the south-west. The modern street in the foreground would have been occupied by houses on the north side of Skinners' Row (now Christchurch Place) in the Middle Ages and the road itself would have been considerably narrower.

way construction, while the earliest Dublin-related medieval texts to be edited were the *Book of Obits and Martyrology of Christ Church Cathedral* (1844) and the *Register of All Saints' Priory* (1845). The first modern recreation of the medieval city, essentially its walled area, was Sloane's map (1882).

Not until the 1960s did archaeological excavations begin to be conducted in accordance with acceptable standards. From then onwards, interest in the city's medieval past was sustained by the work of archaeologists, historians and historical geographers, and by popular support for their activities. Only parts of the past can be recovered from the ground and from documents in practice, but enough evidence is now available to make it possible to recreate at least a sense of the entire medieval city. This is what the exhibition at Dublinia and the contents of this book have endeavoured to achieve.

The crypt of Christ Church Cathedral was built in two stages and underlies almost the entire building. Its design was functional and in medieval times the northern bays fronting John's Lane East were used by stallholders.

Picture Credits

The authors and publisher would like to thank the following individuals and institutions for giving permission to reproduce images: The Board of Trinity College, Dublin, p45; The Bodleian Library, University of Oxford, pp69 (top left), 72 (both) 78, 80 (top), 103; The British Library, London, pp22 (bottom), 25, 27 (bottom), 55 (both), 59 (top), 62, 70 (top), 71, 73 (bottom right), 77, 79 (bottom and top right), 80 (bottom), 81 (top), 85 (bottom), 96 (top), 97 (bottom), 106; The Syndics of Cambridge University Library, pp63 (top right) 88 (top right); Rohan Barnett/Christ Church Cathedral Archives, pp14 (left), 63 (bottom), 67, 114, 118 (top), 122; City of Bristol Record Office, p64 and lock-up and hurdle image on front cover; The British Museum, London, p88 (bottom) and pirates image on front cover; HB Clarke, p52; Stephen Conlin/The O'Brien Press, pp17 (right), 20, 22 (left), 26 (top), 39 (left), 42, back cover; Peter Costello, pp27 (top left), 90, 93 (top); Davison & Associates, Dublin/Christ Church Cathedral Archives, pp1, 6 (left), 69 (top right), 73 (top), 116 (bottom); Davison & Associates, Dublin/St Patrick's Cathedral, pp111, 117 (both); Davison & Associates, Dublin/St Mary's Church, Howth, p30 (middle right); Harry Margary Ltd., London, p50; Department of History of Art, Trinity College, Dublin/Roger Stalley, pp4, 48 (bottom), 73 (bottom left); Dublin City Archives, city seal on front cover, pp3, 23 (left), 56 (both), 58 (bottom), 60, 63 (top middle), 68 (both), 86 (top both), 88 (top left), 91 (top); Archaeology Section, Dublin City Council, pp31, 32 (both), 33 (both); Dublinia, pp6 (right), 8, 9, 10–11, 15, 16 (both), 17 (left), 21, 26 (bottom left), 34–5, 39 (right), 43 (both), 54, 63 (top left), 74, 75, 86 (middle), 93 (bottom), 95 (middle); Dúchas: the Heritage Service, pp18, 23 (right), 26 (bottom right), 27 (top right), 30 (top), 116 (top), 121 (bottom); Friends of Medieval Dublin/Peter Walsh, pp44, 51, 53; Linzi Simpson/Tim Coughlan for Margaret Gowen & Co. Ltd., Dublin, pp30 (middle left), 36 (right), 37, 85 (top left), 87 (top), 92 (top), 95 (bottom), 98, 99 (middle), 100; H & H Design, London, pp82 (both), 84 (all), 85 (drawing); H & H Sculptors Ltd., p110 (all); Musée de Tapisserie, Bayeux, p24 (bottom); Museum of London/Dorling Kindersley, p85 (top right); National Gallery of Ireland, pp13, 29 (left); National Library of Ireland, pp28 (right), 49, 81 (bottom); National Maritime Museum, London, p47; National Museum of Ireland (with thanks to Fennell Photography & John Reid), pp9 (bottom), 36 (left), 57, 70 (bottom both), 76 (both), 83, 86 (bottom), 87 (left and bottom), 88 (top right), 89, 92 (bottom), 94 (all), 95 (top left), 99 (bottom), 101, 102 (all), 104 (all), 105 (all), 107 (bottom), 108, 109, 118 (bottom), pottery faces on front cover; National Portrait Gallery, London, p19; Dan O'Brien, scale-model of Dublin, pp21, 26 (bottom left), 34–5, 39 (right), 43 (left); Royal Irish Academy, pp22 (top right), 48 (top), 52, 97 (top), 121 (top); Colin Rynne/Claire Walsh, p96 (bottom); St Patrick's Cathedral, Dublin, p38; Trinity Library, Cambridge, p107 (top); Robert Vance/The O'Brien Press, p14 (right); Ken Walsh, pp12 and Strongbow image on front cover, 63 (top left), 74; George Walsh, designer of stained-glass windows at Dublinia, made by Irish Stained Glass, pp8, 54; Waterford Museum of Treasures, pp28 (left), 59 (bottom), 61, 65, 66 (top). Thanks to Tomás Redmond, Dublin City Council and Dr Andrew Halpin, National Museum of Ireland for assistance with compiling images.

The authors and publisher have endeavoured to establish the origin of all images used, and they apologise if any name has been omitted.

Suggestions for further reading

Bardon, J. and Conlin, S. *Dublin: One Thousand Years of Wood Quay*. Belfast: Blackstaff Press, 1984.

Booker, S. and Peters, CN. (eds) *Tales of Medieval Dublin*. Dublin: Four Courts Press, 2014.

Bradley, J. (ed.) *Viking Dublin Exposed: the Wood Quay Saga*. Dublin: The O'Brien Press, 1984.

Bradley, J., Fletcher, AJ. and Simms, A. (eds) *Dublin in the Medieval World: Studies in Honour of Howard B. Clarke*. Dublin: Four Courts Press, 2009.

Brady, J. and Simms, A. (eds) *Dublin through Space and Time*. Dublin: Four Courts Press, 2001.

Clarke, HB. *Dublin c. 840 to c. 1540: the Medieval Town in the Modern City*. 2nd edition, Dublin: Royal Irish Academy, 2002. [Large-scale map]

Clarke, HB. (ed.) *Medieval Dublin*. 2 vols. Dublin: Four Courts Press, 1990.

Clarke, HB. (ed.) *Irish Cities*. Cork and Dublin: Mercier Press, 1995.

Clarke, HB. *Dublin, part I, to 1610*. Irish Historic Towns Atlas, no. 11. Dublin: Royal Irish Academy, 2002.

Clarke, HB., Dooley, S. and Johnson, R. *Dublin and the Viking World*. Dublin: The O'Brien Press, 2018.

Conlin, S. *Dublin: One Thousand Years*. Dublin: The O'Brien Press, 1988.

Conlin, S. and de Courcy, J. *Anna Livia: the River of Dublin*. Dublin: The O'Brien Press, 1988.

Crawford, J. and Gillespie, R. (eds) *St Patrick's Cathedral, Dublin: a History*. Dublin: Four Courts Press, 2009.

de Courcy, JW. *The Liffey in Dublin*. Dublin: Gill and Macmillan, 1996.

Duffy, S. (ed.) Medieval *Dublin I: Proceedings of the Friends of Medieval Dublin Symposium*. Dublin: Four Courts Press, 2000. (Series continuing to present.)

Kissane, N. *Historic Dublin Maps*. Dublin: National Library of Ireland, 1988.

McCullough, N. *Dublin: an Urban History*. Dublin: Anne St Press, 1989.

Manning, C. (ed.) *Dublin and beyond the Pale: Studies in Honour of Patrick Healy*. Bray: Wordwell, 1998.

Milne, K. (ed.) *Christ Church Cathedral, Dublin: a History*. Dublin: Four Courts Press, 2000.

Murphy, M. and Potterton, M. *The Dublin Region in the Middle Ages: Settlement, Land-use and Economy*. Dublin: Four Courts Press, 2010.

Pearson, P. *The Heart of Dublin: Resurgence of an Historic City*. Dublin: The O'Brien Press, 2000.

Purcell, E. *A Short History of Winetavern Street and its Environs*. Dublin: Association of Secondary Teachers of Ireland, 1996.

Sweeney, CL. *The Rivers of Dublin*. Dublin: Dublin Corporation, 1991.

INDEX

Numbers in **bold type** refer to illustrations.